RESETTING YOUR LIFE

Unlocking Your True Potential

Randy Wolf

Trilogy Christian Publishers
A Wholly Owned Subsidiary of Trinity Broadcasting Network
2442 Michelle Drive
Tustin, CA 92780
Copyright © 2024 by Randy Wolf

Scripture quotations marked amp are taken from the Amplified® Bible (AMP), Copyright © 2015 by The Lockman Foundation. Used by permission. www.Lockman.org. Scripture quotations marked BSB are taken from The Holy Bible, Berean Study Bible, Copyright (c)2016, 2020 by Bible Hub. Used by Permission. All Rights Reserved Worldwide.
Scripture quotations marked CEB are taken from the CEB® Bible (Common English Bible), copyright © 1976. Used by permission. All rights reserved. Scripture quotations marked esv are taken from the ESV® Bible (The Holy Bible, English Standard Version®), copyright © 2001 by Crossway Bibles, a publishing ministry of Good News Publishers. Used by permission. All rights reserved. Scripture quotations marked (KJV) taken fro The Holy Bible, King James Version. Cambridge Edition: 1769. Scripture quotations marked MSG are taken from THE MESSAGE, copyright (c) 1993, 2002, 2018 by Eugene H. Peterson. Used by permission of NavPress All rights reserved. Represented by Tyndale House Publishers, Inc.
Scripture quotations marked tlb are taken from The Living Bible copyrigh © 1971. Used by permission of Tyndale House Publishers, a Division of Tyndale House Ministries, Carol Stream, Illinois 60188. All rights reserve All rights reserved, including the right to reproduce this book or portions thereof in any form whatsoever.

For information, address Trilogy Christian Publishing
Rights Department, 2442 Michelle Drive, Tustin, CA 92780.
Trilogy Christian Publishing/ TBN and colophon are trademarks of Trinity Broadcasting Network. For information about special discounts for bulk purchases, please contact Trilogy Christian Publishing.
Trilogy Disclaimer: The views and content expressed in this book are thos of the author and may not necessarily reflect the views and doctrine of Tril gy Christian Publishing or the Trinity Broadcasting Network.

10 9 8 7 6 5 4 3 2 1
Library of Congress Cataloging-in-Publication Data is available.
ISBN 979-9-89041-750-3 | ISBN (ebook) 979-9-89041-751-0

TABLE OF CONTENTS

DEDICATION

This book is dedicated to my wonderful wife Kim and our six amazing children: Charity, Destiny, Nate, Christian, Abigail, and Tytus. They have been present during multiple "Resets" and walked alongside of us during those Resets, whether it was starting a church from scratch, becoming bi-vocational as an educator, moving the family from Orange County, California to Scottsdale, Arizona, starting another church in Arizona, or the loss of both parents to working for a Mega-Church. These principles shared in this book have been learned in the steps of the journey; as we have walked through these "Resets" we have gained knowledge that hopefully will speed up your journey and successfully reset your life.

Several years ago we bought a house in Gilbert, Arizona. It was a new build, so the front yard and back yard were a completely blank canvas of dirt. The front yard was small, so it was easy to get to work on that immediately. The back yard was 1/3 of an acre, so the cost and what we wanted to do took some time. Finally, a year later we came up with a sight plan that would include huge, elevated planter boxes with a variety of eight different trees and various kinds of plants. It was a huge undertaking, with 20 tons of dirt, 25 tons of rocks, and an elaborate sprinkler system to water the grass and all the trees and plants. I started the project by having several pallets delivered with large bricks, which I would place on the ground and start to build the wall up to almost three feet tall. I would work on the elevated planter box after I got home from teaching at school and work on it for four hours each night. I would clear the dirt and make sure each brick was level, so as I stacked them they would not fall over. I did this by using a huge leveler on the bricks and the surrounding bricks. Halfway through the project I began to get tired of this process. In my haste to speed it up, I didn't always use the leveler. But shortly after I stacked several bricks, I began to realize I had a problem that affected not only that part of the wall but the other parts surrounding it. Because they were not level, they began to put pressure on the other bricks, causing them to lean the wrong way. If I didn't correct this problem, the wall would eventually collapse under the pressure of the dirt and plants when I put them in the planter box. I had to go back to those bricks I hadn't leveled and reset them, so in the future the wall would stand strong, hold 20 tons of dirt, and multiple trees and plants.

As you read through this book, be sure to apply each principle (make sure they are level) so the surrounding areas of your life will move in sync with the part of your life you are Resetting. May this book take you to a place you have never been and the destination you have longed for in the journey of Resetting your life.

FOREWORD

Randy Wolf's book *Resetting Your Life* is a powerful guide to transformation and renewal. With profound wisdom and unwavering faith, Randy takes readers on a journey of self-discovery and personal growth. His words resonate with sincerity, offering practical insights and spiritual guidance to help individuals reset their lives, embrace positive change, and embark on a journey to a brighter future. This book is a testament to Randy's dedication and passion for uplifting others, making it an essential read for anyone seeking a fresh start and a renewed sense of purpose.

Dr. Dave Martin
Best Selling Author and Success Coach

In *Resetting Your Life*, Randy Wolf navigates the labyrinth of life's complexities, providing a guide for personal transformation. Through a seamless blend of personal anecdotes, scriptural insights, and psychological understanding, this book offers practical steps for emotional, spiritual, and mental rejuvenation. It is more than just a book; it is a timely invitation to reset our lives and reposition ourselves for a fulfilling future—a must-read for anyone yearning for a second chance or a new beginning.

Dr. Terry Crist
Lead Pastor
City of Grace
Mesa | Phoenix | Las Vegas

I've had the great privilege of knowing and working with Pastor Randy Wolf for over 40 years. I can personally testify to the depths of his godliness, faithfulness, humility, and wisdom. In this powerful book, Randy gives us great kingdom insights from God's Word as well as powerful personal antidotes from his remarkable life. Randy has a true pastor's heart and a tremendous teaching gift. Both of those virtues are very evident in every page of this book. When a proven leader, who's a great husband, father, and pastor, pours out his lifetime's learned wisdom and insights, we should all lean in, listen, and learn from them. Lean in! You're going to love and learn from this amazing book! I know I did!

Dr. Michael Maiden
Senior and Founding Pastor
Church for the Nations
Phoenix Az

CHAPTER 1

WHY RESET?

There is a vital feature on Windows operating platforms; it's called "System Restore." This is how it works. Suppose you suffer a system crash on Thursday; you downloaded an infected program or virus…You desperately need to recover the last two weeks of financial information you had saved on your computer on Wednesday, or your daughter's history paper she did on Monday, and you even lost your favorite computer program. All you have to do is select "System Restore" and specify the date to which you want your computer reset. Voila! Problem solved! All the things you somehow were missing are now working the way they should have been.

Have you ever had a moment, event, conversation, or an action you wish you could take back? If only you could reset that moment when things went so wrong. If only there was some way to go back in time and change the way you behaved or the words you said or the action you took!

Wouldn't it be great if you could do that in life, and then be able to make it available for others? You could go back to the day before you got fired from your job and restore; go back to the day before you had that affair and restore; go back to the day before you said those harmful words to your child and restore; go back to the day before you tried drugs for the first time and restore; go back to the day before you made that bad financial decision and restore; go back to the day before you acted in anger and hurt someone and restore. Wouldn't be great if there was a "System Restore" for life's mistakes or painful decisions?

It is said that 30% of an average person's anxiety is focused on things about the past that can't be changed. If we were honest with ourselves, we would all say that there is something in our past that we regret doing and wished we could yell "Do-Over" and find ourselves with a second chance. But because do-overs are not possible we can live in regret and "what ifs". But what if the answer isn't do-overs but a Reset.

One of my moments would be in my sophomore year of high school. The high school I attended was very large. It went from 10th grade through 12th grade, so my sophomore year was like a freshman year these days. I was already taller than almost everyone in my class, so I stuck out. On top of that I was an introvert, so speaking to people was very uncomfortable. I went through most of my sophomore year without saying too much to anyone at all.

My only refuge was basketball, so I trained hard to make the team. I made an alternate team called JV2. It was made up of all the guys that didn't make Varsity, Junior Varsity, or the sophomore team. In my case there were four sophomores in my class that were about the same size, so the coach decided to put one of us on each of the four teams. I was put on the JV2 squad. I was already struggling with my self-esteem, so this impacted it in a negative way. I didn't want to stick out or draw attention to myself, so I practiced hard and kept my head down. It was the first game of the basketball season, and the coach called my number. It was a jump ball at the free-throw line. I went in to replace another player and positioned myself on the arc nearest the opponent's basket. As the referee threw the ball up for a jump ball, the ball was tipped to me. I grabbed it in midair and turned in the air and put the ball in the bucket. It happened so fast; I was impressed how well I pulled it off. Then as I looked over to the bench, the coach had his hands over his face and the players were laughing. It was only then that I realized I had put the ball in wrong basket, scoring two points for the opponent. In that moment, the one thing I had tried to avoid was happening. I had drawn attention to myself, and not in a good way. How I wish I had a button I could press to reset! Sometimes we need a reset because the previous season of our life has come to an end and we need a reset for the new season.

Life today is the sum of the choices we have made. Some of those choices we regret and some of the choices have come to an end and it is time for a new season with new choices. What are some of your regrets? Before you answer that, I want to tell you something…You cannot change the choice or the consequence of regret. No amount of regret will ever allow you to go back and change what has happened.

We sometimes live our lives through the window of regret, regret that we made that choice to marry… work for… become friends with… you fill in the blank. Regretting that choice will not help you avoid making the same choice in the future. Regret will draw you back to that choice over and over again. It has been said that "Regret is like watching life go by through your review mirror." What if we learned to live life through this huge front window instead of the review mirror?

The one thing I know about regret is that regretting something will never help you move forward.

Regretting is a negative thought in motion. Let me explain.

Negative thoughts disturb your interaction with your

environment, affecting your ability to perceive, remember, and reinforce existing neural connections. They cause you to make the same choices by reason of focus.

"For as he thinketh in his heart, so *is* he:" Proverbs 23:7 KJV

The English Standard Version says it this way: "He is like one who is inwardly calculating." Standing over a task saying, "Don't blow it" over and over again is focusing on "blowing it." You are inwardly calculating based on failure, not success. You are focusing on that choice you made which keeps it at the forefront of your thinking. A thought of regret occupies a big part of our creativity and thus influences future action. What you think about a lot will govern how you act, which means you are most likely to make that same choice somewhere in the future.

Here is the good news...you can reset your life to move forward from those events, to orient and orchestrate your future to a positive outcome, no matter what mistakes you have made. You can reset your life so you are ready to move forward and accomplish what God has for you. You need to stop looking back through the review mirror of regret and reset your life and reposition yourself to look forward for what God has next.

The challenge with resetting our lives is that sometimes we don't fully believe we deserve that second chance; we must somehow earn the right to have a "do over." In our thoughts we rationalize that we knew better; we shouldn't have made this mistake; after all, we have been around for a while. Our humanity and our old nature require us to make restitution for our mistake. This thinking keeps us from resetting our lives until we feel we have done enough penance to earn the right to be back in God's favor. We ourselves are our greatest enemy to resetting and repositioning our lives, to moving forward with God.

The reality of this process is found in the word "grace." Grace is the opposite of a "do over;" grace is this attribute of undeserved opportunity to move forward into a place I don't deserve or haven't earned. When we get up tomorrow morning and walk through our day, go to the coffee shop, workplace, eat lunch with our co-workers and connect with our friends, we are to be a living example of God's grace in action to a world that doesn't understand grace. Grace is about God knowing our weakness and failures and yet giving us another opportunity to step into His favor and blessing that we didn't deserve. In providing this grace for all, it points everyone in this world to God and the need of His grace in their lives.

The reality is, when we want a "do over" it is usually for us and not for others or God. "How could I have made this mistake?" The reality that can help you today is, you are vulnerable to making mistakes and will fall short of God's plan for your life, but by His grace you can reset and reposition your life to align with God's will and plan for your life. We didn't come to alignment with God because we earned it, we didn't grow in our faith because we earned it, and nothing was earned as we begin this journey of faith. God's grace says, "I have a plan, a purpose, and a design for your life and I am going to work on accomplishing it." The first action of God's grace was the grace of His dear Son and the life that he has laid down for you in order to bring you into an intimate relationship with God. From that moment on, your life steps into grace, the opportunities to reset, reposition and align your life back to the rhythm of His grace. When we come up short, and we will, we acknowledge the action, ask forgiveness, and His grace moves us onward. We will talk more about this in the next chapter. The challenge is that as the years go by and we make more mistakes, we begin to beat ourselves up about our mistakes. We somehow feel God will be more gracious if He knows how hard we are on ourselves.

When I started playing basketball in high school, I hated to make a mistake so I would verbally beat myself up after a mistake. I believed if my teammate could see how upset I was with my mistake they would be gracious to me and let it pass. We do the same thing with God. We reconcile in our minds, if He sees how upset we are with ourselves He will be gracious to us. But grace doesn't work that way. God is not looking for you to earn a way back into His favor. If He did, no one would make it back into His favor. Jesus has provided the way through our mistakes back to God's favor.

How can we be that example of God's grace to others if we ourselves struggle with accepting that grace in our own lives? We need to get a fresh glimpse into how God sees us and how God's heart is for us and all mankind.

James, the brother of Jesus, knew a lot about the struggle with grace as he grew in his faith, so he writes of the nature of God towards us always.

"Every good gift and every perfect gift is from above, and comes down from the Father of lights, with whom there is no variation or shadow of turning." James 1:17 NKJV

This phrase "no variation or shadow" is a powerful picture of the nature of God towards us. "No variation" means there is no action of changing an orbit. "No shadow" is the time of day when the sun is directly overhead or in noon position. **At noon the sun is directly overhead, the sun rays fall vertically on the body, so the shadow is very short.**

When we put this phrase together, it represents a picture of God, who is over our lives in noon position ready to work and accomplish His will.

God is always in noon position! It is not God who moves from ready position over our lives; we do. We make judgments, say something that hurts another, react to someone's behavior, we close off our lives to someone who hurt us. There are a thousand different ways we could move, but ultimately we said something or did something that moved us out of noon position. In some cases, the previous season is over and God is moving to the new season in our lives so we must move with him. Maybe it is a job and the company is phasing out that division so we need to find another job. This can be a great moment to reset our priorities and goals for the future and what it will hold. In some cases, it can be a combination of the season coming to an end and mistakes we made in the previous season. We need a reset!

We can't take the action back or put the words back in our mouth, but we can reset and reposition our lives back into alignment. We can reset, reset our hearts, thoughts, and actions by what we do next. We can reset ourselves. Then we can reposition our lives back to noon position. Belief is such a powerful entity when it is placed in the right position. We recognize that our words and actions have set some things in motion, but believe that our God can take any situation and redeem it, which aligns us with the plan of God for our lives. I will speak on these in the coming chapters.

We can move ourselves back to noon position, where God is always ready to move forward in His will and purpose for our lives.

Here are some closing thoughts on reset and repositioning our lives.

1) Faith is Required to Reposition Your Life

Faith is choosing to believe that God is still working all things out for His good and that your mistakes haven't disqualified you from His grace and His will for your life. Faith in God and His unchanging nature and promises over your life is required to reposition your life.

Do you see God over your life, ready to accomplish His purpose, or are you still trying to earn a "second chance?" Do you think, "God, if I could just get back to that day, before all this madness happened, before I said those things or did those things"? Realize God hasn't moved behind some cloud, He hasn't moved on to someone else; you have moved. God is still there when we blow it, waiting for us to reset, reposition, and align with Him. God is there when we acknowledge our words and actions, and God is there to restore immediately. God is in noon position in your life, ready to accomplish His good will and purpose. Are you letting yesterday influence your today? God is ready to move in our today and tomorrow, but are we are still trying to get out of yesterday by earning our today? You cannot earn any day you live on this planet; every one of them is a gift from God. You can only choose how you live each day.

2) The Challenge for Resetting and Repositioning is in our Minds

We need to reset our minds concerning God's view of us and our actions. Then we can walk in His grace and move to where we should be to reposition our lives for His will.

We all have perceptions about everything; some of them are true and others are not. As time goes by, these unchallenged perceptions, true or not, become embedded into our minds as a filter for how we see ourselves. If they are not reset and repositioned, they will guide that area of our lives away from noon position.

I have observed this firsthand as an educator, particularly a math teacher. For 20 years I have watched students come into my class with a wrong perception of themselves. I have heard this statement more times than I can remember: "I am not good in math." One particular instance stands out as a reminder that we all need to be diligent in challenging our perception of ourselves.

One day the administrator asked to meet with me. She said there were two students who were failing math big time. She asked if she could transfer them into my classroom from the other teacher's class. She knew I had some success in helping students succeed in math. I met with both students, who informed me "they were no good in math." Prior to meeting with them I went through their student files intensively; I looked at their past grades in math and their Stanford 10 math test scores. I observed that both of them had the skill (they scored well in the Stanford test) but not the mindset to succeed in math. I proceeded to tell them I had seen how they scored before and believed they could succeed in math. I would work with them to make up lost work, but I believed they could pass my class. Over the next several months, after continuing to reaffirm the right belief that "they could succeed in math" and working with them, I watched their grades rise from D's & F's to C's and B's. I helped them reset and reposition themselves in math by challenging a wrong perception in their minds.

What are the wrong perceptions you need to challenge today?

Today is your day to reset and reposition your life!

God loves you and wants to accomplish all His good will towards you and through you while you walk upon this earth.

You are loved of God today; God is ready in noon position over your life to do His good will!

CHAPTER 2

WHAT IS A "RESET"?

The year was 1975 and I was attending a men's advance at Campus Crusade for Christ in San Bernardino, CA that is called Arrowhead Springs. There were over 1,000 men in attendance. I will never forget one of the speakers who spoke at the advance. He wasn't even one of the main speakers but one of those that had shared his story. He was 75 years old; as he got up to speak his face lit up like a Christmas tree. He started sharing about his journey of faith. He told us of how for the last 50 years he had preached in a church every Sunday as the pastor of that church. Upon his 70th birthday something happened: he found Christ. For 50 years he had preached about Christ yet never had a personal relationship with Him. He had followed the pattern of his denomination, gone to seminary and was ordained and preached almost every Sunday. He pastored a good-sized church and for 50 years followed the road set out for him by his professors in seminary, but one day it all changed. One day he really met Jesus through his time in prayer and contemplation of the Scriptures and accepted him as his Savior. He was so overjoyed and filled with peace he couldn't wait to get up Sunday morning and share it with the congregation he had pastored for the past 50 years. He had found the only way to God was through a relationship with Jesus, not by following rules laid out by a denomination. As he shared that morning, he told of his own journey, how he had taught about Jesus but never personally knew Him. But all of that changed, and today he not only knows about Jesus, he has a personal relationship with Him. He ended the service with an invitation for all those there to come know Jesus personally. The church was shell-shocked; they had a vote of the eldership after service and voted him out after 50 years of service to that church. That very moment could have defined his life, but what happened next defined his life and future. He reset, repositioned, and aligned with God's plan for his present and future. He started another church at the age of 70 and for the last five years he had preached with more passion and vitality for life than the previous 50 years. He said the last five years were the most fulfilling years of his life. He had personally seen many people surrender their lives to Christ over the past five years, that they were the most fulfilling time of his ministry. He teared up as he shared that a life without Christ is not really living, and as long as God gave him breath, he would continue to share the good news.

A "do over" for the past 50 years was not what he

needed; he needed a "Reset," to reset his life to a new beginning with a different way of living to a new destination. To be quite honest, a "do over" will eventually end up at the same place as before. You are doing the same thing again, with the same thoughts, the same attitudes and in the same way, hoping to arrive at a different outcome. We all tell ourselves, "Well, if I have a 'do over' I won't make the same mistakes." In reality we make the same mistakes because we haven't changed the starting point, the thought patterns, the belief systems, and the attitudes. We have only told ourselves we won't make that mistake again.

A reset life is the most fulfilling life you will ever live!

I will never forget this story as long as I live; this guy was a living example of how it is never too late to reset our lives. It is a story of how each of us can open up to God and resolve our past which will put us immediately back in the center of God plan, because God is always in noon position. He could have gotten bitter; he could have lived in regret over the past 50 years, but he chose to reset and repositioned his life. Now he was celebrating the past five years of his life and what God had accomplished in that short time.

At any given moment in the journey of your life, you can reset your life; it doesn't have to be because you messed up. I truly believe our lives will be filled with many moments of reset. To identify those moments and then take the right actions is so crucial to moving forward and not getting stuck in the previous chapter of your life. A career may be ending and it is time for a reset to a new career, a relationship may be ending and it is time to reset what you will look for in the future with a new relationship. A reset gives you a fresh start, a clean canvas to paint a new story, a new beginning to make new choices to plot a new destination.

Today the word "Reset" is being used everywhere. "Reset your life, come to our Spa."

"Reset your life, fly to a new destination." "Reset your metabolism, try our new product." "Is it time for a marketing reset?" "What is a soft reset?"

The "Reset" we are talking about begins by finding your center. Finding your new center is the first step to resetting your life. Think of your center as the place where things are perfectly balanced for you. That place is different for each of us. Finding your center allows you to be accepting of the good and the bad in life and understand that things are always changing, but that center helps your feel more balanced and grounded when things are difficult

You find your center by asking some vital questions, like, what do I want the new to look like? Who would I want in this new reality? Where do I want to be three years from now? How do I want to see life going forward? What do I want to do differently this time around? What are some of the attitudes and thoughts I want to leave behind?

That center becomes your new starting point, your reset beginning, aiming at a new destination; it becomes your reposition place in life with new goal, new behaviors, new thought patterns and new attitudes.

The Bible is full of stories about people that needed to "Reset" their lives. Let's look at the story of Jacob, who got out of position in life in a huge way and needed to reset and reposition his life so it would align with God's will.

Jacob was the second son of Isaac and Rebekah. He was a twin but born just after his brother Esau. They grew up as two distinct and different brothers. One loved hunting and the outdoors; the other loved cooking and creative things. They look very different in appearance as well. Isaac loved Esau more as the oldest. The oldest in their tradition inherited twice the inheritance of any other sibling; this was called the "birthright." As Jacob and Esau grew older, the story tells us of an event that happened one day. Esau is out hunting for quite some time and returns at the brink of starvation. His brother has made an amazing stew. Esau asks Jacob for some and Jacob replies, "Give me your birthright and I will give you some stew." Esau responds by saying, "What good is my birthright if I die? Let's trade my birthright for some stew." It is here we get a glimpse into their family and sibling relationship. Jacob wants to be Esau, he wants to have what Esau has, from family inheritance, to family blessings, to a father's approval. Much later in this story as Isaac is very old and at death's door, Jacob with his mom's help comes up with a plan to steal the father's blessing. He makes a stew (something about Jacob's stew), dresses in an animal skin so his dad will be deceived as he touches him (because Isaac is legally blind) to think he is Esau and bless him. Jacob is 77 years old and still wants someone else's life. You never outgrow your insecurities, but you can "reset" from a life affected by them. For the last 77 years Jacob has wanted to be someone else; he has wanted what someone else has and has never stopped to see the value in his own life. He has this drive within him that is based on a belief that if he has someone else's life he will feel at peace, fulfilled and satisfied. This is what has driven his behavior for 77 years. Now because of everything he has done he has to run for his life. Jacob runs for his life because he knows his twin brother will kill him for what he has stolen. He runs roughly 460 miles from where Esau is.

Mostly likely Jacob is feeling the weight of his decisions and wishing he could go back and change things or have a "do over." I can only imagine the thoughts running through his mind. "Why can't I just be happy?" "Why did I behave so badly with my twin brother?" "Why wasn't my father more involved in my life?" "What will I do now?" "Have I lost everything I fought to get?" "What will the future look like to me now?"

He is so exhausted mentally and physically, at night-time he lies down in the desert and uses a stone for a pillow. Can you say "really tired"?

It is in this moment Jacob so needs to "Reset" his life.

Resetting your life is a profound and transformative process that involves intentionally breaking free from the patterns, beliefs, and circumstances that have defined your past and present.

Jacob has beliefs based on his circumstances (he was born second, not first, his father loves Esau more, if he is more like Esau he will gain his father's love, blessing and acceptance). These beliefs have caused him to develop a life of deception in his behavior toward Esau and his father.

Reset is a courageous act of self-awareness and reflection, where individuals reassess their goals, priorities, and values, allowing them to realign their path with their true aspirations. Resetting one's life often entails letting go of old baggage, overcoming fears, and embracing change as a means of personal growth. It provides an opportunity to start anew, casting aside self-imposed limitations and societal expectations.

Jacob needs a new start, one unencumbered by his past beliefs and behaviors.

Reset is an act of renewal which allows individuals to forge a fresh direction, cultivate new habits, and foster a greater sense of purpose and fulfillment. In essence, resetting one's life is an empowering journey of self-discovery, paving the way for an authentic and more meaningful existence.

In his journey, Jacob realizes the vast difference from what he pictures life would be like from his choices to the place he has wandered. In this place of his own decisions, he has no vision of the future, no roots from the past, and he feels lost in the present. In this desert place he has come to the realization that he needs a "Reset." There is no pathway home and no future pathway that he can see. As long as we keep coming up with solutions to the dilemma we face by our choices, we will never see the need for a "Reset." We will spend our energy trying to come up with every possible action for a desired outcome without re-aligning to a new pathway with new habits, new thoughts, and new patterns.

All of Jacob's efforts and choices have brought him to the brink of mental, emotional, and physical exhaustion. It is illustrated in this story by the words "taking one of the stones there, he put it under his head and lay down to sleep." You have to be utterly and totally exhausted to fall asleep on a stone.

As Jacob falls asleep, he has a dream of angels descending and ascending on the place where he is at. God then speaks to him about who he is, what God is doing for him. and what God will do for him and finishes up by telling him God is with him now, with him where he goes, and will one day bring him back home.

In this waking moment Jacob begins the courageous act of self-awareness and reflection on how he has ended up in this place, but he is also beginning a new journey with new goals, values, and priorities, one that is filled with new beliefs, new attitudes, and new behaviors. His starting point is not where he grew up; his new starting point is here in the desert, in this place where he had a vision that begin the "Reset" of his life.

Let me say it again, Reset is an act of renewal which allows individuals to forge a fresh direction, cultivate new habits, and foster a greater sense of purpose and fulfillment. In essence, resetting one's life is an empowering journey of self-discovery, paving the way for an authentic and more meaningful existence.

As you follow the life of Jacob, he has several additional "Resets" as he sees the self-imposed limitations put upon his life by fear, failure, comparison, and the limitations put on his life by others and their opinion of him.

What are the fears, failures and comparisons you have imposed on your life?

What are the opinions of others that are still dictating your life?

It is time for you to awake to the potential of your life and the amazing opportunities that lie just around the corner, just out of your sight.

CHAPTER 3

RESETTING FROM UNDER-VALUED

There are many reasons why we need to reset our lives; some we have listed in the last chapter and there are many other reasons too numerous to list here.

We could try to put them into categories to help us formulate a better response for the need to reset. Three main categories seem to stand out more than any of the others. First, we find people need to reset their lives because of some action or deed they did that messed up their lives, marriage, family, occupation, friendship etc. Second, they undervalued their lives and by recognizing the gifts within them and they have now outgrown that past setting or where and who they work for undervalued their lives and through learning their gifts and abilities and growing those gifts they have grown past the value others have placed on them. Third, they have experienced some sort of sudden hardship or loss that requires them to change. In this chapter we will unpack this second category; we will look at a key life skill and a story of how we tend to undervalue our gifting and abilities which cause us to settle into a life that is less than our potential, or how others have put us in a box and we have grown and don't fit there anymore. Maybe you find yourself there today. I am not talking about a committed relationship like marriage. In that case you must upscale your marriage to grow with your giftings. I am referring to other areas where you have awakened to the reality that you don't fit in that career, job, or friendship anymore. You have grown in your giftings and you have outgrown where you are. You feel a shift needs to happen, but I submit to you a Reset needs to happen, a Reset in which you have shifted to a place where you can be you in the full potential you have realized and there is no ceiling.

Every life on this planet is a gift from God. Each life has been given gifts and abilities by God to do some amazing things. Today we must stand up against the devaluing of each individual life. The individualism of humanity is a beautiful tapestry and design of God. Each life is ordained with a plan, purpose and gifts and abilities to leave a lasting mark on this generation and the next and the next.

Imagine with me for a moment that a cure for cancer is within an 8th grader struggling to find some value for their life as he/she is being made fun of or bullied in junior high school because they are different. What if we could tell him/her "You have God-given gifts/abilities within you, and as you walk/journey through this life you will discover those gifts/abilities and you will leave an amazing mark on your generation!"

Look at this passage in the Bible:

Matthew 25:14-15 NLT: "Again, the Kingdom of Heaven can be illustrated by the story of a man going on a long trip. He called together his servants and entrusted his money to them while he was gone. He gave five bags of silver to one, two bags of silver to another, and one bag of silver to the last—dividing it in proportion to their abilities. He then left on his trip."

Look closely at the last part of this passage.

"...dividing it in proportion to their abilities" - everyone possesses some abilities from God,; not one human life exists without some abilities from God! The silver given in this story to each person represents the opportunities to use these God-given gifts/abilities to leave a mark on this generation and the next.

You were not designed to live life never understanding what you possess as gifts/abilities from God, never realizing what is on the inside of you, what you are capable of doing. To see your life as just plain, of no significance, just ordinary and without distinction, is to allow yourself, others or life's circumstances to devalue what you possess.

Socrates said, "The unexamined life is not worth living." This is only half true. We need to examine and have an accurate assessment of our lives. The unexamined life still is worth living, it is just unfulfilled. Within every individual is a sense, almost like a quiet voice telling us we were made for more. To ignore that voice, or to let life or others quiet that voice, is to live with a sense that I/you were made for more. This sense can lead us to look everywhere else and never examine our lives to see what is within. I need a new job, a new spouse/life partner, a new car, a new... you fill in the blank. This search becomes endless and unfulfilling in the long term. The beginning point is to acknowledge we were made for more, with gifts/abilities given by God for some greater purpose, some divine purpose.

This is echoed in Ecclesiastes 3:11 AMP:

Ecclesiastes 3:11 "...He has also planted eternity [a sense of divine purpose] in the human heart..."

Each individual has within them "a sense of divine purpose," a quiet but relentless voice calling us to discover what our divine purpose is by uncovering what gifts/abilities God has designed within us.

As we uncover what gifts/abilities are within us, we begin to discover our divine purpose.

What does this journey of uncovering look like?

Many times we tend to look at our lives by what is apparent, in front of us, and make an assessment of what we can or cannot do. This will always leave us coming up short, because many of those gifts/abilities are waiting to be uncovered as we journey through life. They are not evident at once but can take years to discover. They are based on the right circumstance, the right opportunity, the right connections, the pressure to move outside our comfort zone, the right timing and being open to discover, to name a few.

Julia Child is remembered for her love of French cooking and her TV show that brought fine cuisine to the masses. But before she churned out exquisite recipes on camera, she made a career as an intelligence officer working under the agency that preceded the CIA. Early in her life she wrote the following assessment of her life. Child barely showed any special interests other than a vague ambition of becoming a writer. In her diary she wrote, "I am sadly an ordinary person...with talents I do not use." Julia Child wanted to help the country prepare for World War II. She tried to join the military; she was rejected from both the Women's Army Corps (WACs) and the Women Accepted for Volunteer Emergency Service (WAVES) because she was too tall. In 1942, she became a senior typist with the Research Unit of the Office of War Information in Washington, D.C., and, by the end of the year, Child was a junior research assistant with the Secret Intelligence Branch of the Office of Strategic Services (OSS), the precursor to the Central Intelligence Agency or CIA. Julia Child was placed at multiple stations abroad during her career as an intelligence officer with the OSS, including Kandy, Sri Lanka, where she met her husband, Paul Child, a fellow OSS officer. After the couple married, they moved to Paris, France. It was during their time in France that Child, whose privileged upbringing left her with no cooking skills, became enamored with French cuisine. She enrolled in Le Cordon Bleu, one of France's most prestigious cooking schools. It was an ambitious undertaking since, as Child put it herself, she could only "boil water for tea." "Really, the more I cook the more I like to cook. To think it has taken me 40 yrs. To find my true passion," she wrote to her sister-in-law.

Julia Child worked in advertising, media, and secret intelligence before writing her first cookbook when she was 50, launching her career as a celebrity chef in 1961.

Imagine if Julia had stopped with the assessment, "I am sadly an ordinary person…with talents I do not use." Imagine if the rejections she got along the way were the measure for her life. Imagine if she let her past define her future – she could only "boil water for tea."

The journey to uncover these hidden gifts/abilities within us begins with recognizing we have not discovered all that is within us yet, so let us journey to new discoveries.

It begins with this first step, having an accurate way to measure what is within us. This is the starting point.

Look at this passage from the Bible found in Romans 12:3.

"As God's messenger I give each of you God's warning: Be honest in your estimate of yourselves, measuring your value by how much faith God has given you." TLB

From this past story we can see this process of "measuring your value" is a vital skill set that can release you to uncover hidden gifts/abilities.

What is this process?

It begins by challenging the self-restraining, limiting beliefs you have about yourself or others have about you that have influenced you to believe a certain way about yourself.

This is seen in the early life of David.

David is the youngest of eight brothers. They were warriors and he took care of his father's sheep. One day a man called Samuel came to their house and asked the dad, Jesse, to gather all his sons so Samuel could observe them. Unknown to them, Samuel was told by God that one of Jesse's sons would be the next king of Israel. Jesse gathered seven, leaving David in the field, after Samuel realized that someone was missing Jesse called David to come home. When David walked into the house Samuel knew that David was the one. Samuel spoke a prophetic word over David and anointed him to be the next king. From that moment on David's giftings and callings outgrew his present situation. The problem existed because David's brothers and others tried to keep him in the same place and role. David had to escape the restraining and limiting beliefs of others.

This played out so clearly in David's life when he voiced objections to Goliath mocking the nation of Israel.

First his brother tells him to stay in his lane; he is only a shepherd. 1 Samuel 17:28 CEB:

> *When David's oldest brother Eliab heard him talking to the soldiers, he got very mad at David. "Why did you come down here?" he*

said. "Who is watching those few sheep for you in the wilderness?"

Then he is told by Saul he is unable to resolve this problem. 1 Samuel 17:33 CEB:

"You can't go out and fight this Philistine," Saul answered David. "You are still a boy. But he's been a warrior since he was a boy!"

Everyone has a place they believe you would best fit and they want to keep you there. These are restraining beliefs placed on you by others. This is what they did to David. They had beliefs about David's giftings and callings and wanted to keep him in the place they believed he would fit best. When this didn't work they tried to limit David with limiting beliefs by placing him in Saul's armor. Saul said, "Wear my armor." Each man's armor was designed to fit that man perfectly so it could protect them and allow them to move quickly in battle. This was so important, because if it didn't fit perfectly they could die from open spaces in the armor or they could not move quickly and would die.

Are you believing and wearing someone else's limiting beliefs (armor) about yourself? Listen to the words of David.

1 Samuel 17:38-39 CEB:

> *Then Saul dressed David in his own gear,*
> *putting a coat of armor on him and a bronze*
> *helmet on his head. David strapped his sword*
> *on over the armor, but he couldn't walk*
> *around well because he'd never tried it be-*
> *fore. "I can't walk in this," David told Saul,*
> *"because I've never tried it before." So he*
> *took them off.*

David said "I can't walk in this." David no longer fit in the value they had placed upon his life, he outgrew it as he recognized his giftings and calling. "So he took them off." It is time for you to take off others' limiting beliefs about who you are and what giftings and callings you possess. They may mean well, but you can't walk in their opinion of you or what you should be doing any more.

He no longer fit the ideas and plans others had for his future, so David had to Reset to the new value of his life. He outgrew his past setting and needed to Reset to new, wide-open places.

This happened several times in David's life.

David speaks of this in Psalms 19:18:

> *He (God) brought me out to wide-open*
> *spaces; he pulled me out safe because he is*
> *pleased with me. CEB*

You are not in a midlife crisis, you are in need of a Reset to wide-open spaces where you can thrive without the restraints of other peoples' opinions and ideas about what you should be doing.

Julia had to challenge the self-restraining belief she had about her abilities and passion to cook.

"Really, the more I cook the more I like to cook. To think it has taken me 40 years to find my true passion."

What do you believe about yourself, or what others have told you, that it is time to challenge instead of accept as truth?

Second you must refuse to accept your past or present state as your future. This is easier said than done; many times we are unaware of the limitations we have put on ourselves. It may have been years ago, and by now we have lived with those limitations without challenging them but accepting them as truth. If Julia had accepted her ability to only "boil water for tea" (her past) she would have never enrolled in Le Cordon Bleu (her future). What have you accepted from your past or now as your future?

Next, we recognize how important it is to try new things without the fear of failure. Today fear of failure has kept many people from uncovering hidden gifts/abilities.

The inner dialogue within us sounds something like this: "What if I fail? If I fail, then if means I found another thing I am no good at. And if I fail then I am a failure." All of this is self-defeating and not necessarily true. To try new things is to expand your horizons, to discover what you might be good at and yes, you might not be good at that one thing, but you can move on with confidence knowing you are closer to uncovering what you are good at.

Next, once you discover a new gift/ability, you must give yourself to that gifting to discover the depth and height of that gift. Maybe it is writing, designing, teaching, speaking, playing an instrument, negotiating, selling some product, etc. There are some practical ways to do this; first, begin to learn everything you can about these new gift/abilities. I would do this by studying those with similar giftings. For speaking I would watch and learn how others had mastered this gift, not to be like them (because we don't need another one of them, we need you, the original individual) but to learn how they are presenting that gift. If it is teaching, watch them on YouTube to see how they teach. In addition, take a class or several on expanding that gift. Take a class on public speaking, writing, negotiating, designing, or selling through many avenues. Those classes will expand your vision and thinking into what is possible. Finally, find a mentor who is in that field and ask them for advice on how to develop, market, and expand your gifting. We can save ourselves valuable time and energy by avoiding mistakes and learning valuable lessons from those who have walked a road similar to ours ahead of us.

Lastly, value doesn't come from what you have or haven't accomplished yet butvalue comes from confidently utilizing that gift to the highest potential for what the gift/ability is able to do. Comparison is the killer of dreams, visions, and confidence. When we compare ourselves with others, we use the wrong metrics to place value upon our lives. I learned an important lesson years ago, to measure my performance not by what others did or in comparison with what others have accomplished, but did I give it 100% in this present moment. What 100% looks like will change as you grow in that gifting/ability; it will expand and increase as you faithfully steward that gift/ability.

The whole story is found in Judges chapters 6 & 7. We will be looking at Judges 6:11-15 NLT in the Bible.

[11] "Then the angel of the LORD came and sat beneath the great tree at Ophrah, which belonged to Joash of the clan of Abiezer. Gideon son of Joash was threshing wheat at the bottom of a winepress to hide the grain from the Midianites. [12] The angel of the LORD appeared to him and said,

"Mighty hero, the LORD is with you!"

[13] "Sir," Gideon replied, "if the LORD is with us, why has all this happened to us? …

[14] Then the LORD turned to him and said, "Go with the strength you have, and rescue Israel from the Midianites. I am sending you!"

[15] "But Lord," Gideon replied, "how can I rescue Israel? My clan is the weakest in the whole tribe of Manasseh, and I am the least in my entire family!"

From this story we can see that Gideon in his present state was a terrified young man just trying to survive. He was hiding from the enemy, just trying to gather enough wheat to feed himself. If we ran him through a leadership assessment for today, nothing, I mean nothing, would call out to us "This guy is a future leader." His personal assessment might look something like this; Gideon is a young man who possesses a number of fears, he seems to be a loner, keeps to himself, possesses few skills of value, comes from the most insignificant tribe of the 12 (not one of the original 12 tribes), his family is the most insignificant family in this tribe, and Gideon is the youngest in his family. In our humble estimation Gideon will not achieve much and will probably not amount to anything significant.

Can you imagine what it would be like to live with this assessment by everyone? From this account of the story, we can see Gideon believed what life and others had said about him. Gideon was living with limiting beliefs. He fully accepted them, never once challenging them, and if not for a reset he would have lived his life out following this pathway. What pathway are you on that is far below the value of who you are? Who has told you what you are and are not? Who has overlooked you because you don't fit their perception of a leader? You are more than their perception, you are more than their ideas, you are more than the value they spoke over your life. It is time to reset your value to the right value of who God has made you to be and the gifts/abilities He placed within you. It is vital to the way you will live your life.

We can see here in this story that the value of our lives we accept is the way we will live our lives. Gideon saw his life as a life of survival, just trying to make it through another day. He is so convinced of that, that when a divine being shows up to contradict that assessment he argues with the divine being.

Hidden within this story is an amazing moment, one we will mostly miss. This divine being showed up and sat under a tree before he ever engaged in a conversation with

Gideon. One might be quick to think he is watching Gideon, thinking, "This guy is such a hopeless case; he is living so far below his capacity." I think he is watching him saying, "I really like this guy; I don't see him as he sees himself. When Gideon really sees who I have designed him to be and the gifts/abilities I have already placed within him, he will reset his life and step into his purpose. When Gideon sees what he is capable of doing and what he possesses he will make a lasting imprint." I see this by the statement this divine being makes to Gideon after a while of silence, "Mighty hero" He addresses Gideon by who he really is and what he is capable of doing long before Gideon ever does a single thing. He starts by resetting Gideon's value of himself, because Gideon has so devalued himself based on what others have said and what his circumstances have dictated. This divine being realizes that somewhere along the journey of life Gideon's value of himself was skewed and greatly lowered. We can only assume how that might have happened. Maybe by what he encountered growing up, he was the last in a tribe that had no significance. He never had opportunities to really step up like those around him, so he just settled for whatever came his way. Maybe by what others said, they reminded him of where he was from. That no one of great value ever came from the tribe of Manasseh, that his humble family was no the leader type. Maybe they went so far as to say, "Gideon, you are average in school, so just find a good average job and build and average life." Maybe by the hard path he walked in life; he is just trying to gather enough wheat to feed himself. Where is his family unit that stands with him, supports him and comes to his aid? He is out there by himself, trying to survive today and just make it to tomorrow. Do you find yourself within the story of Gideon? Struggled with academics, not the best upbringing, being told you were just average, coming from what may be an insignificant past not marked with memories of success.

One thing is evident in this story and in your story: Gideon had the wrong value placed on his life, which caused him to head towards the wrong destination and come up way short of what he was capable of doing. And so do you!

Somewhere, Gideon's life was undervalued and he accepted it as truth and now believed that fact. Again, as we talked about this earlier in this chapter: the first step was to challenge that limiting belief and to reset Gideon's value of his life.

In a moment God challenges Gideon's belief and value of his life. "Mighty hero, the Lord is with you!" God would say something similar to you today, "Mighty hero, mighty song writer, mighty designer, mighty entrepreneur, mighty leader, mighty schoolteacher, etc." Not just hero, but mighty, which points to a depth of gifting/abilities to leave an imprint on his generation. It is time for you to see everything within you! Stop saying "I am just..." You are filled with great potential (mighty) to make a mark today!

Gideon tries to dismiss this valuation of his life by where he is at right now. "If God is with me, why has all this stuff happened to me?" Here is an important point to resetting your life and the second thing Gideon had to do. (Again, we pointed this out earlier in this chapter.) You have to move past your past, and what is happening right now to step into the purpose God has for you.

Colonel Harland Sanders. An icon. A legend. A failure. That's right, a failure. Colonel Sanders had to put in some seriously hard yards before his Original Recipe Chicken finally spread its wings across the world. Harland Sanders took his first job painting horse carriages, then another working as a train conductor. He practiced law for three years in Little Rock, Arkansas, then got a job selling life insurance. After that he started a ferryboat company - why not?! Then he cashed that in to set up an acetylene lamp manufacturing business. Next, he opened a string of gas stations. That didn't go so well. Harland Sanders took over a service station in 1930, where he began serving weary travelers the same fried chicken he grew up eating. As he began to advertise his food, an argument with a competitor resulted in a deadly shootout. Four years later, he bought a motel which burned to the ground, along with his restaurant. Yet this determined man rebuilt and ran a new motel until World War II forced him to close it down.

Following the war, he tried to franchise his restaurant. His recipe was rejected 1,009 times before anyone accepted it. Sander's "secret recipe" was coined "Kentucky Fried Chicken," and quickly became a hit. However, the booming restaurant was crippled when an interstate opened nearby, so Sanders sold it and pursued his dream of spreading KFC franchises all across the country.

After years of failures and misfortunes, Sanders finally hit it big. KFC expanded internationally and he sold the company for two million dollars ($15.3 million in today's money).

Where would KFC be today if Sanders let the past and the now determine his future? How many tines did Harlan have to move past what just happened and keep grinding? He didn't let what happened to him affect what he believed about the gifts/abilities within him. Each time he faced an obstacle he "reset" and moved into the future.

In the story of Gideon, God remined him of two things.

You have never seen yourself as a leader, but you are!

"Go with the strength you have, and rescue Israel from the Midianites."

There is something already in you, Gideon, the strength and gifting. You don't have to try and muster up the gifting; just discover it right now. It was within Gideon the whole time, all the time while he was living in fear and survival mode because of limiting beliefs. He was living so far below his value and capacity. He didn't "measure his value" correctly.

The second thing God reminded Gideon was that God was with him, so give yourself 100% to this gifting/ability.

God's reminder to Gideon is found in Judges 6:14—"I am sending you!"

Gideon goes out later in the story after a "reset," fully believing, discovering, and 100% engaged in his gifting/abilities, and blows a trumpet to all the tribes of Israel (a call to gather for war). 32,000 men of war came out to follow Gideon the leader. For years Gideon had been living under a wrong value, accepting what others said about him and never assessing the gifts/abilities within him. After a "reset" he stepped into his giftings/abilities, led the nation into a phenomenal victory over Israel's enemies, and brought freedom and peace to a generation. His story was written and recorded for all generation to see and to inspire us all to correctly "measure our value." Your future is waiting. Others are waiting. This world is waiting for your mark.

Every one of us will struggle with times of insignificance, does my life really matter? But in those moments, it is vital we remind ourselves that within each of us is something special, and if we courageously walk through this moment something amazing will happen in our future.

Transitioning through this reset is not easy, but necessary. To awaken to the reality that you have gifting and abilities presently not utilized to their full capacity is the beginning point. The transition is to reset yourself and build from this new starting point. The challenge is that family, friends, coworkers, and others are used to the other you. They may struggle to embrace this new you and even try to dissuade you from moving forward. They mean well, but have not had the awakening you have had and still see you in the light of your old value. The key component to reset is to continually remind yourself of the "real value" of your life and the gifts you possess as you walk through the process. One day it will be evident to them as they see the manifestation of your inner beliefs and giftings.

Like in the stories of Julia, Harlan, and Gideon. Their walk through the process of reset and the evidence of that reset is now history, as they have left a mark in their generation. The same is true of you. So discover who you really are!!

CHAPTER 4

RESETTING FROM HARDSHIP

In this chapter we will look at the need for a "reset" when hardship arises. Sometimes that hardship leaves us with loss; loss of a loved one, loss of a job, loss of a marriage, loss of a child, loss of career, loss of a friendship, loss of health, loss of a good name. You fill in the blank: loss of _____.

Hardship will touch us all; at some time and place we will face some challenge that will become a crossroad in our lives. The pain of that moment will seem overwhelming. It can leave us feeling frozen in time and wondering, "How do I move forward or can I move forward?"

At that moment we will need the understanding of:

How do I move from this place?

How do I not let this moment define the rest of my life?

How do I find some pathway to a new destination?

How do I honor that person or place and still move forward in life?

How do I deal with this moment?

Hardship and loss can leave us with more questions than answers.

In this chapter we will identify some steps we can take to help us move forward beyond hardship and loss, and Reset our lives to a new destination, one that honors our loved ones but also moves us forward.

Life can turn on a dime, and when it does, it is important we know how to "Reset" our lives to move forward from that moment. Our dreams and hopes for our perceived future can shipwreck our lives if we don't embrace the "Reset" to a new perceived future. This new perceived future is one we never saw coming but one that is here nevertheless.

Such was the case for Jon Scheyer.

In Illinois in 2004, the lights were on at the gym at Glenbrook North High School as the sun rose. Inside the facility, 17-year-old Jon Scheyer began what had become a daily routine, getting shots up and starting his day with basketball.

A full school day came next, followed by the team's practice, which went to roughly 6 p.m. Scheyer and his teammates headed back to their homes, and while the day began to wind down for most high school kids, he still had work to do. His mother, Laury, had dinner on the table and conversation ensued with her and his father, Jim. After homework assignments, the day finished the way it started — with the orange ball and the smooth sound of nylon.

Scheyer would hop in the car to head to nearby Bannockburn Health Club and Gym to close the day with a workout on the hardwood.

He had one thing on his mind: win a high school state championship for his community. That's what his roots meant to him, and after a third-place finish as a freshman and an Elite Eight run as a sophomore, coming up short of the high school state championship title as a sophomore became a driving factor for his off-season training his junior year.

There were plenty of avenues for Scheyer to take for his high school playing days, but he had pride in where he came from and wanted to deliver hardware to Northbrook. He went to Glenbrook North, where he was coached by Dave Weber, the brother of then-Illinois head coach Bruce Weber.

When it came to Scheyer's recruitment, the buzz only increased after he led Glenbrook North to a state championship as a junior in 2005.

It didn't necessarily start great for Scheyer at Duke, as his four-year playing career in Durham featured its share of adversity. He was named an All-ACC Freshman, but the Blue Devils scuffled to an 8-8 record in the conference, losing four straight games to close the season, including a heartbreaking defeat to 11th-seeded VCU in the first round of the 2007 NCAA Tournament.

The following year, Scheyer was the sixth man on a 28-6 squad,

Everything came together in his senior season, though, as he put together an All-American campaign and lead the Blue Devils to a national championship, averaging 18.2 points and 4.9 assists along the way. He climbed the mountaintop and etched his place in a Blue Blood's history books.

Scheyer went into the 2010 NBA Draft with some momentum, and he was projected as a second-round pick by multiple outlets.

But two months later, the road got bumpy. Scheyer went undrafted, but agreed to a deal with the Miami Heat's summer league team. In the first action in Las Vegas, he hit the game-winning shot. In the second matchup, everything turned for the worse in an improbable fashion.

Scheyer was poked in the eye by Golden State's Joe Ingles, but it was not just any casual basketball injury. The setback was life-changing, as the optic nerve in Scheyer's right eye was avulsed and he suffered a tear to his retina. Just when it looked like his career was about to get going at the next level, Scheyer found himself in a hospital bed, wondering if he would ever be able to play at the same level.

Following the eye surgery, Scheyer dealt with headaches and had to wear an eye patch. It was a tough road back, and his depth perception was changed. In February 2011, after recovering throughout the fall and winter, Scheyer agreed to a contract with the Rio Grande Valley Vipers, the Houston Rockets' D-League team.

Scheyer toughed it out for the Vipers, averaging 13.1 points, 4.0 rebounds and 4.0 assists in his D-League season. That said, if he was going to have a productive next basketball chapter in his professional playing career, it was going to have to come overseas. He agreed to a two-year deal with European League powerhouse Maccabi Tel Aviv, spending two years in Israel before heading to Gran Canaria in the Spanish League for a season.

"Any major success that I've had in my life, I've failed first," Scheyer said. "You can go to my high school career, my college career or even dating my wife. I got lucky for a second chance with her."

The eye injury never allowed Scheyer to find a lasting pathway to the NBA, but it led him to coach.

"It's amazing looking back. What a pivotal moment in my life. You think your life is heading in a certain direction, and all of a sudden, you feel disappointment that it didn't work out. Then, two months later, you're going this way,"

Can you say "Reset?" Reset from the dream of playing NBA basketball to being a coach.

I can only imagine the process of "Reset" in Jon's life to a new dream or goal with new hopes and a new perceived future.

In this chapter I don't in any way want to minimize the impact and weight of hardship and loss on your life. Some of you have faced great loss and are still feeling the weight of that. Some of you are still processing what that loss means to you and others. I realize you will need time and space to come to terms with that loss. This chapter is about taking some steps when you are ready to move forward, when you fully grasp you can't go back, you can't have a "do over;" you can only move forward.

I can't imagine what that moment felt like to Jon Scheyer, when he realized everything he had been working for, everything he had sacrificed for and everything he had hoped for was now gone, followed by thoughts of, "What do I do now? My whole life has been laid out on this pathway, working towards this goal and future and now it is all gone." What once was so clear and achievable is gone. Yesterday you were moving toward the goal, today you were blindsided and left wondering "Where do I go now, what do I do now?" Now looking back the distance you traveled towards that goal or perceived future seems so empty. All the work you put in over the years seems wasted in this moment.

We all make plans based on what we think will be the natural progression of our lives. We will get married, wait five years while we buy a house, then have two children. Then hardship or loss happens and the natural progression is gone. We find out we can't have children, what now? Our plans and steps toward that goal are halted, leaving us to wonder "Why did this happen?"

I have sat across the table with many a soul that is walking through a similar loss. I have struggled to find the right words and feel so inadequate with my empathy, knowing the weight of loss is weighing heavy upon them, knowing that in this moment no words can bring full release to their souls. In that moment everything feels final. So many emotions flood the soul as they try to process what has just happened.

Like a ship without a compass how do you steer your life forward with no clear direction?

In that moment when life fell apart it left you feeling lost in your journey.

On January 17, 1994, a massive earthquake hit Northridge. This earthquake killed 60 people, injuried more than 9000, and caused damages in the amount to exceed $20 billion. But it also altered the journey of millions. It caused seven highway bridges on the Santa Monica Freeway (I-10) to collapse. This freeway runs from Houston to Santa Monica. For 74 days, millions of travelers had to re-route their journey. The collapsed bridges left them with no clear path to their destination. They had to come up with other plans to get where they were going. Hardship and loss are like that earthquake in Northridge; they come unexpectedly, they jar us, leaving us unsure, and there are aftershocks that keep us off our game and emotionally on edge. The damage they do leaves us with no clear path to our destination; we find ourselves grasping at alternate plans in a confused state.

My wife and I have struggled with loss in our own lives. What was once so clear and the steps so achievable is now gone. We had built a life, we had two wonderful children, amazing friends who believed in our goals and were a part of the journey, we were on our way to what was going to be an amazing ride. But setback after setback has left us with no more options and no clear pathway to our goals. The weight of that moment felt overwhelming and final. It left us questioning, was it all just a pipe dream? We had so many questions.

How do we keep from being stuck in this moment of unknown, wondering how we move forward so this doesn't become the place we stop in life, wondering how we move our family forward so it doesn't leave an impression in our children lives that alters their perception in the wrong way?

Every year in October across this nation people are setting up Fall Festivals. Usually these Fall Festivals are on a farm with lots of space. On the farm they have so many different booths and rides, but the one I don't like is the dreaded corn maze. I always approach it with the confidence and faith that this time I will make it through. I begin to plot my way through before I even enter the maze; I see so clearly what steps I should take and how I will successfully navigate my way through. I even account for some unexpected turns, knowing that if I stick to my plan I will succeed. When I have felt I have it all planned out and can visually see the route I am going to take, I enter the maze and begin my journey. Inevitably I find myself stuck, and the route I planned out seems to have some unexpected delays and dead ends. As I stand before this dead end, I can feel in the moment that I am never going to reach my goal. The visualization in that moment is lost. I think life is like that. We plan out our steps, set our goals, account for unexpected turns we think will happen, and mentally see/manifest the results. Then we begin the journey with confidence, vision, and faith. But then just like the maze the unexpected that we didn't see coming or happening, happens. There in that moment the vision/manifestation is lost. We find ourselves lost without a clear vision on how to proceed and wondering howwe reach our goal. All our planning, all our steps, all our visualization is gone. Instead of confidence, we just want to get out of here.

There was a time in history of the Nation of Israel where their continued bad choices over many years led them into a season of hardship and loss. They had lost their homes, lost their communities, many of them were uprooted and transplanted in another country. When they arrived there, they believed they would go back home soon, they believed that things would go back to the way they were, that this moment was just a momentary setback. But as time passed from the initial loss so did their hopes and dreams. Seventy years later, God spoke a word by way of the prophet Jeremiah to the nation, a word to help them Reset from their loss personally, relationally, spiritually, financially, and emotionally.

Jeremiah 29:11 AMP "For I know the plans *and* thoughts that I have for you,' says the LORD, 'plans for peace *and* well-being and not for disaster, to give you a future and a hope."

God was saying, "I know the past loss is weighing heavy on your hearts and minds and you have believed that this is all your future has to offer. I know that your minds have accepted this and now you believe that your loss is final, but it is time to RESET! I have a future and hope that you haven't seen beyond your loss, I have a future and hope that I want to take you to. But you must RESET from that past season of loss to a new season of 'peace and well-being.'"

Part of the process leading to a Reset after hardship and loss is to process the loss and disappointment we are now dealing with and take time to let ourselves feel the weight of that loss. Each person is different, and each person will process that loss and hardship differently. Give yourself the space to be you and how you move through that loss and hardship. There are three things we can do to move us toward that Reset moment in our lives.

First, we must learn to make peace with what has happened but not let it be a voice of finality. Some ways that can help make peace are talking with an expert or a friend or family member, writing down our thoughts by journaling, and by not trying to rush through this moment. There are some great books out there that have some amazing strategies on how to deal with all the emotions you are feeling from that loss or hardship. Sometimes reading someone else's story gives you hope and strategies on how to navigate your own loss. Each one must be open to the pathway that best works for you. Just because someone suggested what worked for them does not mean it will work for you. Try a few of these options or try them all to see which are the best for you.

Secondly, we need to recognize that life is going to have sudden unexpected disappointments. So we need to build into our lives the skills to handle adversity and disappointment. These skills are valuable to our present and future.

Those skills are Emotional Management (the ability to express your emotions in a healthy way), Acceptance (the ability to accept those things you cannot change), Patience (it takes time to navigate through the steps of this adversity and disappointment), Confidence (the ability to face this situation believing you can make it through). These last three (Acceptance, Patience and Confidence could be defined as "Resilience."

Jon Scheyer said, "For me, I've learned to handle adversity well. It doesn't mean there's no anger or frustration, but I do get back up and keep fighting." Those lessons we learn going through hardship and loss will become vital for us to handle the next moments of adversity.

Jon Scheyer's first season as Duke's head coach, 2023, was filled with a lot of ups and downs. They had some very disappointing losses to Wake Forrest, NC State, Clemson, Virginia Tech, Miami, and Virginia. His own journey helped him lead the team through those difficult losses and Reset to what was possible. They ended up going 16-0 on Coach K court. They did really well in the NCAA tournament. No lesson learned or skill gained in navigating through adversity is ever lost; it sets us up for success in the future.

Thirdly, we need to recognize just because is over...

(you fill in the blank) doesn't mean there isn't something in your future. What you're saying and thinking matters. Today there is a lot of emphasis on "manifesting." Manifesting is a self-help exercise that refers to focusing your thoughts, feelings, and beliefs on a desired outcome.

Fill your moments with positive thoughts and positive self-talk. Positive self-talk can help a person feel encouraged, motivated, and optimistic. Self-talk refers to the internal dialogue that goes on in your mind, and it can have a significant impact on your mood, your mindset, and your ability to cope with difficult situations. We will talk more about this in the chapters to come.

These three things will bring you to the moment of Reset.

That moment of hardship and loss may seem like eternity, finalization, and the loss of all hope, but there is a moment that is about to happen next. There is a moment beyond that moment; there is a new pathway somewhere just out of sight.

What you have endured has brought you to this point, to this moment, and now you realize it is time to Reset to a new destination. Reset our lives to a new destination one that honors our loved ones but also moves us forward to a new perceived future, one we never saw coming but one that is here nevertheless.

CHAPTER 5

RESETTING YOUR LIFE FROM A MAJOR MISTAKE

In this chapter we will explore how to Reset your life because of some action or deed you did that messed up your life, marriage, family, occupation, friendship etc.

There is a story about a guy named David. David had everything one could want and hope for in life and then made a series of bad choices that made for a huge mess up.

We can use his story as a guide for us today on how to reset and reposition our lives to be in alignment with God. We can see the steps he took to place himself back in noon position with God.

David came from a large family. He had seven older brothers and two sisters. David did not look like his brothers in size and stature because he was still young. They were grown fighting men and their stature impressed the Prophet Samuel. David was still growing into his frame at the time of Samuel's visit. When Samuel anointed David as the next king it was an unlikely and unperceived "Reset" of David's life. David was a shepherd boy who

God called to be king of Israel. Years later he became king and saw God's favor and influence upon his life and the kingdom. He had all but conquered his enemies. He had everything his heart desired, beautiful palace, beautiful wives, children, fame and fortune, position, and power. Sometimes all the fame, fortune and power in the world is not enough to quiet the voice of insecurity in our lives. The one that is still trying to overcome our upbringing and the lack of love, favor, acceptance, friends or position _____ (you fill in the blank). It might be good to note here that many of the mistakes we make are to gain something we really don't need to fill some void we have within our hearts and lives. One night David unable to sleep, wandered out onto the roof and watched a beautiful woman bathing next door. He begins to desire what is not his and his thoughts begin to lead him on a pathway to many bad choices. He proceeded down a pathway on his way to violating four commandments. Look at this passage of scripture from the Bible.

2 Samuel 11:1-26. He coveted his neighbor's wife, then he slept with her, committing adultery, then he found out she was pregnant so he tried to cover it up by bringing back her husband, Uriah, from a battle on the front lines, but her husband would not go sleep with his wife because he felt it would be wrong to enjoy life while his fellow sol-

diers were still fighting on the front line. So David sent him back to the front lines with a message to the commander to put Uriah on the front lines of an assault and then pull back so he is killed in battle. So David had Uriah killed.

David violated four commandments on the way to getting what his soul wanted, what he needed, what he thought he couldn't live without. David is out of position with God for what God wants to do in his life. Today many of us are out of position with God for what God wants to do with our lives. Our mistakes may have slowed the process, but our actions can get us back into position with God.

As time went on, David was separated from God by his own mistakes. David lived this way for many months, out of position, doing his own thing, separated from God's plan for his life. Are you living out of position with God for your life?

David had walked a certain way that led him away from God for many months, at least nine months, maybe more. That whole time God was wanting David to return, to come back to Him. But David continued to live out of position with God and God's plan for his life. David accepted these unchallenged perceptions that "I can live any way I see fit and still be in noon position with God." He would have probably died believing these perceptions if he wasn't confronted and challenged on his actions and beliefs.

Confronting a wrong perception is the second step in resetting your life. Unconfronted wrong perceptions will continue to guide our lives because we believe them to be true.

Only after being confronted by Nathan did David deal with his actions.

Today is your day to Reset your life; what is it that you haven't dealt with?

As we talked about in the second chapter, Reset is an act of renewal which allows individuals to forge a fresh direction by the courageous act of self-awareness and reflection, where individuals reassess their goals, priorities, and values, allowing them to realign their paths, cultivate new habits, and foster a greater sense of purpose and fulfillment. In essence, resetting one's life is an empowering journey of self-discovery, paving the way for an authentic and more meaningful existence.

Nathan is the tool to force self-awareness and reflection upon David. He comes to David and confronts him over his sin in the form of a parable. Then Nathan said to David, "You *are* the man!" — 2 Samuel 12:7.

The result of David's action was the loss of a life. The

child born to him and Bathsheba died seven days after it was born. What happens during those seven days and after is a blueprint for us on how to reset our lives. What David did was to reset his heart, reposition his life, and align himself for blessing. I know I am jumping ahead here, but I need you to see the blessing that lies ahead for you.

The story goes on to say David had another child with Bathsheba.

> *"Then David comforted Bathsheba, his wife, and slept with her. She became pregnant and gave birth to a son, and they named him Solomon. The LORD loved the child."*

> *"...and sent word through Nathan the prophet that his name should be Jedidiah—'beloved of the LORD' —because the LORD loved him."*

— 2 Samuel 12:24-25

David did something that Reset and repositioned him back in the purpose and will of God. How can this be? David had violated four commandments, he messed up big time, yet now God said "We're good." David understood the process; he reset his life to a new center and he said to God, "I've done wrong, I've messed up big time, (self-awareness and reflection) I'm going to recenter my life and I'm going to get myself repositioned back with God." And God said, "We're good to go; let's move on with what I have for you and your life." David got a fresh start, a clean canvas to paint a new story, a new beginning to make new choices to plot a new destination.

This wasn't the only big mistake David made; he made several other mistakes after this one. Each time David dealt with his mistakes by acknowledging them, taking full responsibility for those actions; Resetting and Repositioning himself back in the will of God for the purpose and plan of God for his life. This is what God loved about David: his ability to reset and reposition himself with God and move forward with God after messing up. When David died, God said, "Put on his gravestone 'A man after my heart.'" God knew David, like all of us, would mess up many times, but that is not how his/our lives our measured. They are measured by our ability to do what needs to be done next.

This is where many get stuck. We want to fix the mistake by going back and doing something to make it right. But many times we can't undo what has been done. David couldn't make Bathsheba unpregnant, he couldn't bring Uriah back to life. He couldn't fix the choices he made that caused this horrible mess up. Sometimes you can do something to help heal the wounds but that will be a part of the reflection process. What needs to be done next is to reset our lives, reposition our lives, and bring our lives back into alignment with a God in noon position over our lives.

Now let's closely look at what David did to reset his life.

When David's child died, he could have gotten bitter, he could have gone into a depression, he could have blamed someone, he could have quit on life and got stuck. There were many paths he could have taken from those mistakes he had made and where they had led him. David was one decision away from favor of God and God's will for his life.

You are one decision away from God's favor and will for your life.

He needed to reset his life, and in 2 Samuel 12 NKJV it records how he moved forward, how to reset after a deliberate action of wrong, how he Reset himself into the purpose and plan of God for his life.

2 Samuel 12:18:

> *Then on the seventh day it came to pass that the child died.*

2 Samuel 12:19:

> *When David saw that his servants were whis-pering, David perceived that the child was dead. Therefore David said to his servants, "Is the child dead?" And they said, "He is dead."*

2 Samuel 12:20 NKJV:

> *So David arose from the ground, washed and anointed himself, and changed his clothes; and he went into the house of the LORD and worshiped. Then he went to his own house; and when he requested, they set food before him, and he ate.*

"David arose from the ground" – being on the ground was a position of full humility and repentance (this is the place of self-awareness and reflection). It is a heart bowed to God as the Supreme Being with full acknowledgement in our wayward hearts that we have wandered from His path for us. In its truest sense, it is not bargaining with God but accepting what has come our way and wanting God to show us mercy instead of what we deserve.

This idea of repentance has been misunderstood and overused. Repentance is a reset of our lives back into con-nection with God, His plan, and His purpose and moving forward from there. Repentance is acknowledging fully the action or actions we have allowed to come into our lives and move us from noon position, to separate us from God and His plan for our lives. Repentance is wanting one thing: to have our lives restored to God and His plan and then moving forward to accomplishing that in our lives. This is where David is during this seven-day process, owning up to his actions which led him from God's plan and asking God to be merciful to him and his child.

This process of repentance is a heart process; it goes to the center of who we are (it is centering our lives) and who we are supposed to be. This heart process goes beyond feeling sorry for my actions and the results my actions have caused. It goes to the place of wanting complete change, never wanting to do this again. Feeling sorry lasts but a moment and then I move on to make the same mistake again, I never reset my life. I just hit a bump in the road and then continue along as if nothing has happened.

My son and I were driving to school one morning on the freeway when we heard a loud bang. We were traveling about 65 mph in the carpool lane and immediately looked around to see what caused the noise. Had we hit something? We noticed that a truck two lanes over was trying to straighten itself out after noticeable swerving. The truck had hit a bump in the road that caused it to jump sideways for a second. As we looked over, the truck continued on is journey as if nothing big had happened. The next moment was so unexpected. Just then the back bed of the truck began to fall off, being dragged by the truck. This created an even louder noise than the first one. When the driver hit the bump, he should have slowed down, pulled to the side of the road, and examined his truck for any damage done by the bump, but instead he continued along as if everything was normal.

When we hit a bump in the road we should slow down, pull to the side of the road, and examine what just happened. This process is called repentance (self-awareness and reflection). Repentance must start in the heart and then proceed to our thoughts; it is allowing our hearts to deal with the bump/mistake, own up to it, examine the effects, and wanting from the center of our hearts not to do it again. One of the definitions of repentance is to reconsider morally and to think differently afterwards. It means to perceive and change the seat of moral reflection that implies altering the course of your life to a new direction. It is resetting your life to the path of God from your own path.

We need to understand this journey that David took away from God by his actions. This process is called sin. We need to understand what sin is and how it affects our lives, how it alters our path from the path of God to an alternate path away from God. The word sin means to miss the mark. It is the picture of an archer shooting for a target and missing the target. The archer could have just missed the target by an inch or he could have missed it by 100 yards, but either way he missed the target. Sin means we have missed the target God had for our lives in that situation. We behaved wrongly in a certain situation, we spoke harshly in a certain conversation, we judged another wrongly, we acted with the wrong intentions. There are so many ways to miss the target, but ultimately we missed the target. No amount of bargaining, penitence, or minimizing will resolve the results of missing the target. Our need to classify sin becomes a part of this equation. We say, "My sin was not as bad as Joe's, Michael's, Sarah's", etc. In doing this we miss what sin does; it separates us from God's purpose and will for our lives. How far you missed His plan is irrelevant. The process back it the same for all. The process to Reset is called repentance. When my children come home with a bad grade and begin to justify it by saying "Everyone in the class did bad," or, "It's better than most of the class," my response is to lovingly point out that they are not doing what they are capable of doing. They have missed what they were designed to do, and no comparison will make it right.

Your actions and my actions separate us from God's plan and will for our lives. It temporarily moves me from the center of God's will and plan and halts the movement of God from accomplishing His will for my life. A reset is necessary to get me back to where I/you need to be. And a reset always begins with repentance.

There was a time in the nation of Israel when they were wondering why God's will and plan wasn't working in their lives. Their conclusion was, God is not strong enough to help them or God could not hear their prayers. God answered their response and tells them this is a wrong conclusion. This conversation gives us great understanding for what our sin does to our relationship with God and His will for our lives.

Isaiah 59:1-2 NLT:

> *Listen! The LORD is not too weak to save you, and he is not becoming deaf. He can hear you when you call. But there is a problem—your sins have cut you off from God.*

Our actions can separate us from God's will and plan for our lives. Secondly, this breach in our relationship with God hardens our hearts towards God.

In the desert we have riverbeds that get really dry and cracked when we don't get enough rain. They are no longer functioning the way they were designed. They were designed to carry water downstream to plants and vegetation and cause the area to flourish. When our lives stop carrying water and become dry, they harden up and we exist but stop flourishing as we were designed to do.

The longer we remain on our own path taken by our sin/actions the harder our hearts become toward the will and purpose of God. Repentance is about the heart; it goes to the center of the heart, who we are and who we are supposed to be. Repentance restores our hearts back to God. David spent seven days in repentance because he had allowed his actions to separate him from God for 9-14 months. His heart had become hard by living outside God's design and will for his life. When my computer freezes up and will not function as it was designed to, I need to go to the power source and shut the computer off. This is called a "hard reset" and sometimes like in the life of David he needed a "hard reset." He stopped eating, he stopped working, he stopped everything to get humble before God and "hard reset" his heart back to God.

Sin/mistakes cause the God-designed melody for our lives to go flat or sharp. And if the God-designed melody for our lives goes flat or sharp we need to retune/reset our lives to His melody. Repentance is taking time to in humility to tune our lives back to the rhythm of God for our lives.

In junior high I played in concert band. Before each practice we were expected to tune our instruments to perfect pitch before we began practice. This required us to spend some time tuning our instrument up by ourselves. Quite frequently, someone got lazy or showed up late for class, so their instrument wasn't in perfect pitch. The teacher would hear the noticeable conflict of sounds as we practiced. She would stop and ask each instrument individually to play a certain note, and then in front of everyone she would tell us if we were flat or sharp. God wants us to constantly tune our lives to His perfect pitch for our lives, to spend time each day making sure we are in sync with Him. If we become lazy or delinquent, He may have to tune us up in front of others. His desire is never to point us out mistakes but to make sure we are in the right place so what comes out of our instrument matches the melody He has designed for us to play. This is what happened with David. He didn't tune up his instrument and continued to play out of pitch, so God had to do it in front of others, because God loved David too much to let him continue to play out of tune. And God loves you just as much, so He will not allow you to continue to play out of tune for too long without adjusting you.

The second bell of the Westminster chime is tuned to B-flat and the third bell is tuned to middle C. Some years ago, musicians noted that errand boys in a certain part of London all whistled out of tune as they went about their work. It was talked about and someone suggested that it was because the bells of Westminster were slightly out of tune. Something had gone wrong with the chimes and they were discordant. The boys did not know there was anything wrong with the peals, and quite unconsciously they had copied their pitch.

Repentance tunes up our flat and sharp lives to the perfect pitch of God's heart.

Repentance resets our lives to the rhythm of God's will and plan for our lives.

This process may take a little time if we have allowed our hearts to become hardened by living in that sin for a while. It doesn't take but a moment for God to forgive, but it may take a little time for us to acknowledge and own up to our sin from our hearts, not just our minds and mouths.

David immediately acknowledged his sin when confronted by Nathan.

2 Samuel 12:13 NKJV:

So David said to Nathan, "I have sinned against the LORD."

David was saying "I have sinned" – I accepted the choice I have made as my own – it has affected my life, the lives of others and my relationship with God.

During those seven days David was letting the Great Designer of his heart tune him back to the melody God designed his heart to live in, to reset his heart.

In a remote Swiss village stands a beautiful church - Mountain Valley Cathedral. It has high pillars and magnificent stained-glass windows, but what makes it special is the most beautiful pipe organ in the whole region. People would come from far off lands just to hear the lovely tunes of this organ. One day something went wrong with the pipe organ. It released the wrong tones and produced sounds of disharmony. Musicians and experts from around the world tried to repair it. No one could find the fault. It was made unique, customized, and no one really knew how to fit it. They gave up. After some time, one old man asked, "Why isn't the pipe organ used?"

"It's not playing right," said the church staff.

"Let me try." Since it had been lying there, the staff

reluctantly agreed to let the old man try his hand at it. For two days the old man worked in almost total silence. The church worker was, in fact, getting a bit nervous.

Then on the third day - at noon – suddenly the music came. The pipe organ gave out the best music after so many years. The people in the village heard the beautiful music. They came to the church to see. This old man was playing at the organ. After he finished, one man asked, "How did you fix it? How did you manage to restore this magnificent instrument when even the world's experts could not?"

The old man said, "It was I who built this organ fifty years ago. I created it, and now I have restored it." - James S. Hewett, *Illustrations Unlimited* (Wheaton: Tyndale House Publishers, Inc, 1988) pp. 244-245.

During those 7 days that acknowledgement worked its way to the center of his heart. Listen to the words of Psalm 51 that was recorded during this time of his heart reset. David's first words are to ask God for mercy.

Psalm 51:1

> *Have mercy on me, O God, because of your unfailing love. Because of your great com- passion, blot out the stain of my sins.*

Psalm 51:3-4

> *For I recognize my shameful deeds— they haunt me day and night. Against you, and you alone, have I sinned; I have done what is evil in your sight.*

Psalm 51:6

> *But you desire honesty from the heart,*

Psalm 51:7-8

> *Purify me from my sins, and I will be clean; wash me, and I will be whiter than snow. Oh, give me back my joy again.*

Then David ends this heart cry with what he really wants: he wants to be back in noon position with God. David wants to be reset to the rhythm of God for his life and fulfill God's plan and purpose for his life.

Psalm 51:10 NLT

> *Create in me a clean heart, O God. Renew a right spirit within me.*

God promises us that if we will own up to our actions, acknowledge of those mistakes and surrender our hearts, He will forgive us and cleanse us immediately and restore us to noon position.

1 John 1:9 NKJV:

> *But if we confess our sins to him, he is faithful and just to forgive us and to cleanse us from every wrong.*

This means God will remove all record of that mistake and action. In the eyes of God, it is a done deal and we are good with Him.

God wants to reset us and reposition us immediately, because God is always in noon position.

Faith is nourished in the promise of God and nature of God who will do what He says, no matter our mess-ups.

At the end of this seven-day process of heart restoration, David's heart and life are reset through heart repentance and he is ready to reposition his life and take the next step in the will and purpose of God.

CHAPTER 6

PERCEPTION IS EVERY-THING; WHAT DO YOU SEE?

What does it mean to reposition yourself? Why should you reposition your life? How can one reposition himself? What is the process of repositioning? We will discuss many of these questions in the coming chapters. Let us look at what it means to reposition yourself.

In the last three chapters we have identified three of the top reasons to Reset your heart. From all three of those places, we must now reposition our lives to grow into our future with no hinderances.

Reposition means the position you have been playing the last several months or years is not the position God ordained you to play, or maybe that position has come to the end of its season and it is time for a new position. Comfortability and personal preferences play a big part in what we will settle for and what secondary role we will play. We can live a certain way for so long it seems right, but that does not make it right. Things in our lives are constantly changing, and many times we adapt to fit into those changes. We change jobs and give up family time to become a success, we make new friends and start going out every night to keep those friends, we have marital problems so we spend more time at work which leads us into an unhealthy attachment to a coworker. We adapt so much that we find ourselves out of position for God's plan for our lives. God wants to reposition you for the new day and new future He has for you!

Between 8th grade and 11th grade I grew significantly, from 5'8" to 6'6". In junior high school I played the 4th man position in basketball (today it is called power forward). In high school, as I grew to be 6'6", my basketball coach had me play the post position or the 5th man position, with my back to the basket. Throughout high school I had to learn a new way to play basketball. I learned to play the game with my back to the basket, posting up on the defender. I learned six different moves from this position. I used my size and height as an advantage to be successful playing this way. This was great for the level of competition I was facing, but when I moved up to the next level of competition, college, this positioning would no longer be successful. The success I had in the last season would not translate to success in the next season. In college I was too short to play the post position anymore; the guys playing that position were 6'9" to 6'11". I was shifted back to playing power forward or the 4th man position. The power forward plays most of the game facing the basket, taking the man off the dribble or rising up to shoot over the man guarding him. It took me a whole year to relearn how to play the game of basketball from a different position. I had learned how to do things one way, which now no longer worked as I changed positions for this new season of life. I had been repositioned to another position. I had to Reset my life and reposition my play to a new way of doing things. I now needed to learn how to play the game from that new position. I had to change my thinking, my perception, my movements, and my approach to the game from this new position. It took me a year to reposition my thinking and change my position, but through hard work, consistent practice, and learning new skills, I learned to play the game from a different position. It is time for you to learn to play this game of life from a different position. Things have changed; you have been reset to a new starting point. God is raising you up to a new level that requires a new positioning to play the game of life at this new level. Here is the reality: you have been reset to realize you need to be in a different position for this new season. You might be out of position for what God has for you tomorrow.

Let's look again at the story of King David.

David has lived out of position for 9-14 months and

learned how to live that way. He had adapted his life to play out of position for so long it felt comfortable and right, but he wasn't in the position God wanted him in for his tomorrow. It was now time for him to reposition his life to live differently, to learn to live a new way, the way God had ordained him to live in this new season and moving forward.

2 Samuel 12:20 NKJV

So David arose from the ground, washed and anointed himself, and changed his clothes; and he went into the house of the LORD and worshiped. Then he went to his own house; and when he requested, they set food before him, and he ate.

David arose…

The word arose means to stand up, come about, to bring to fruition. It denotes a movement to an erect position, an upright position. It suggests the beginning of an action to rise up…to position, to stand, to life, to favor, to battle. This word is used to express resurrection as arising from death.

David arose from the completion of repentance, reflection, and revaluing his life; his heart was now reset to a new place. Now he needed to move forward in the plan and will of God to a new position. David had reset his relationship with God in the process of repentance; now David was arising to reposition his life to move forward with God.

It is time for you to arise from your reset to reposition your life to move forward in the will of God. It is time for you to arise to the greatness of God, to the plan waiting for you, to the destiny you were born to live.

The repositioning begins with arising. Arise to a higher position than your last one, a position of favor. It can be that resurrection from loss or hardship that you have just come through. It can also mean that in the last season you were in a position that fit that last season but now in this new season you're out of position for this next season. So you must arise to this new position.

After arising, David did a series of defined things in a specific order. The thing David did next represent a thing a person does that wants to reposition himself to live in a new day.

2 Samuel 12:20 NKJV,

> *So David arose from the ground, washed and anointed himself, and changed his clothes; and he went into the house of the LORD and worshiped. Then he went to his own house;*

*and when he requested, they set food before
him, and he ate.*

These four things symbolize some amazing things that can be a template for us to follow.

Arising from the ground, washing oneself, anointing oneself and changing clothes; all these things together symbolize making a new beginning by repositioning your life.

When I see these four things I am immediately drawn to 4 ideas which we will discuss in the next several chapters. The first being washing himself. David arose from his lower position of repentance and washed himself. He removed the smell of the last season, he removed the sight of the last season, the effects of the last season and he repositioned himself. Washing oneself I see as a changing of our perception.

David realized the perception from the previous season would keep him in the previous season. It was a perception of Resetting the heart, so it required humility, repentance and coming to the reality that the previous season is over; I must move forward. This new season is a season without those same perceptions but a repositioned perception.

By washing himself, he was washing away his old perceptions and moving to a new vantage in which to view life. *Perception* means we make different evaluations of different information that comes in, based on how we are looking at it.

> **"You have the ability to paint a picture of what your life is going to look like. For better or worse, what you envision often begins to take shape. Be intentional and choose to envision a life of significance, possibility, and impact."**
>
> Tony Dungy, from his book
> *The One Year Uncommon Life Daily Challenge.*

Your perspective today has a lot to do with what happens tomorrow.

Perception isn't something that occupies our thinking very much, but it has a huge impact on our lives. Our perception defines who we believe ourselves to be, how we believe we should treat others, and how we believe this world should function. Perception defines for us what reality we will see and live in. Perception takes information that is gained from our senses (touch, sight, hearing, smell, and taste) and interprets that into a conclusion. The most powerful of our senses is sight. Sight, many times, is the first indicator of our perception which becomes our reality. Perception becomes more important than reality. If someone perceives something to be true, it is more important to them than if it is factually true. Perception is our view of reality. Our perceptions influence how we focus on, process, remember, interpret, understand, synthesize, decide about, and act on reality. In doing so, our tendency is to assume that how we perceive reality is an accurate representation of what reality truly is.

What is your perception informing you of today? Is your perception unconsciously trying to get you to make up for the previous season? Have you challenged that perception? What reality are you living in today that may not be true? How has that reality formed your life today?

As we saw in the last chapter, David was in a state of repentance (acknowledging and owning) over his past mistakes. Now that process has come to conclusion; the result of those mistakes has caused the death of his newborn son. Through this time of humility and acknowledgement he has reset his heart from the course it was on. In this moment he can choose to adopt a perception that has put him in this place. He can choose to believe it as his reality, "I have blown it big time with God and His favor is no longer with me." It was a great run but that is over now and I must just learn to make the best of it. Maybe it isn't a mistake for you but you have been doing life at a certain level but it is time to step up into a new level and yesterday's perception cannot take you to this new level. Maybe you are still wishing the loss or hardship in the previous season hadn't happened so you are focused on how to protect tomorrow from that same loss Those perceptions will actually keep you functioning at the same level no matter how hard you try to rise. Maybe you find this to be true if you have moved from an employee of a company to a manager, or from a manager of a company to a part owner of the company or a part owner of the company to owning the company. Each of these progressions will require a new perception to function successfully in that new arena. For example: as an employee you can strive to be everyone's friend, to get along with everyone even if someone is not doing their job, but as a manager you will need to see (new perception) that trying to be everyone's friend will keep you from seeing that some people are better served in a different job. That for the sake of the company and their own sake staying in that job where they are not thriving can be hurtful to them and the company.

Throughout my years as a student, I seemed to struggle with English class. In 10th grade, because of my struggles with English, they put me in remedial English class.

Remedial English class is a course that covers sentence-to paragraph-level writing. Basic remedial English also covers the vocabulary and reading comprehension skills necessary for successful college-level work. They felt this would help me catch up with my classmates. In 11th grade I again struggled in English class, so in 12th grade they put me back into a remedial English class. As I left high school, I had the perception that I would never do good in English class, so why should I try anymore? I felt like English and writing would never be my thing so I headed into college towards a degree in mechanical engineering.

When I went to college, I dreaded taking English class, but was required to take one for my degree. I thought, "Here we go again; I am setting myself up for failure and I am going to hate every minute of this class." The second semester I had a choice and found a class called "creative writing." I hate English and writing but at least this is the lesser of two things I hate. When I went to class, I was surprised by the way this class functioned. We were told in this class to just write our thoughts without concern for grammar or spelling. My perception changed and I found myself loving the ability to write down my thoughts without the struggle of figuring out if it was correct grammacticly or how it was spelled. Without the restraints of the past, I was able to form a new perception, one not based in my past struggles or failures. Today I would definitely not be writing anything had my perception not changed and I realized I could write something that might help others. And thanks to amazing editors who can help with grammar and spelling.

It is time for you to rise to a new perception, one that will carry you into a new season. Remember, perception is how you choose to see things. Most of the time this is formed by past experiences, good or bad. To change your perception, you must see things from a different vantage point, through a different lens. To change it you must first take note of your vantage point. How are you presently seeing things? This is easier said than done. Most of the time we don't recognize that the way we have seen things in the past is forming the way we see things in the present. Unconsciously, we are thinking, acting, and behaving a certain way because of a past perception we are still living in. So even though we are given new avenues to walk in, we still process those avenues through the perception of our previous season.

How can we intentionally change our perception?

There is a story that has great insight on how to do this. There was a man whose name is Abraham; he is married to a beautiful lady and has built a very successful business. But he has one desire that is unfulfilled. He and his wife have not been able to have children; they have tried so many times but without success. For years they have lived with the unfulfilled hope that this time might work. When he was 75, he and his wife got a promise from God that they would produce "a great nation." Now, 10 years later and after a lot of false hope they are still without a child. The reality they have experienced has shaped their perception. It can be seen in this dialogue with God and Abraham.

"But Abram replied, 'O Sovereign LORD, what good are all your blessings when I don't even have a son? Since you've given me no children, Eliezer of Damascus, a servant in my household, will inherit all my wealth. You have given me no descendants of my own, so one of my servants will be my heir.'" Genesis 15:2-3 NLT

You can hear it in Abraham's voice, "You (God) have given me no children" so "this will never happen and I and my wife are left with only close friends."

Abraham is filtering his life through this perception; "left with only close friends" must be what God meant, not one born of my own flesh. No amount of words will change that perception. Something greater is needed to lift him to a different vantage point: visualization.

A lot has been written about visualization and manifestation. Visualization is the act of picturing something you imagine. Everyone is able to visualize. Close your eyes for a second and think about your favorite cuisine or something you enjoy, maybe a donut or a chocolate brownie. Now take a whiff and feel the thrill of your first bite. It is very easy to visualize something you are familiar with, but it takes a great deal of ingenuity to visualize something that your mind has no reference to. Manifestation is impossible without visualization.

So how does God overcome this link in Abraham's life? Visualization through a known to an unperceived.

"And the LORD brought Abram outside [his tent into the night] and said, 'Look now toward the heavens and count the stars—if you are able to count them.' Then He said to him, 'So [numerous] shall your descendants be.' Then Abram believed in (affirmed, trusted in, relied on, remained steadfast to) the LORD!" Genesis 15:5-6 AMP

God takes Abraham outside of his tent. Abraham's tent is symbolic of his safe zone. His safe place, his place of the known, his place where things make sense, the predictable place. For 50 years, inside this tent it was Abraham and Sarah, no children, no heir. Even though God spoke to Abraham, his perception was shaped by where he lived, the environment he spent his life in. Before God could change his perception, He had to bring Abraham out of the tent into a wide-open space to reframe and enlarge his perception. What is God trying to bring you out of that has shaped your perception and kept you from stepping into all that He has for you? What is God quietly speaking to you to set the stage for a perception shift? As long as you remain in the same comfortable environment you have been in for the previous season, you will filter every new word through that season. God is trying to move you out of your safe, comfortable, predictable place.

Abraham has lived inside this world of perception for so long it has framed his very existence. To reposition him, he must leave the confines of a comfortable, safe place to wide-open vantage point. It is in this wide-open vantage point that Abraham can imagine again. When we are kids we have vivid imaginations, but as we grow older we learn to give our imagination lesser value and space. As we learn more about the world around us and what is or isn't possible, it affects our creativity and we settle for what has been experienced. For the last 10 years, since the promise, Abraham and Sarah have experienced barren-ness and they have tried to come to terms with the false hope of having children. Repositioning Abraham outside his known safety zone is crucial to help him Visualize and manifest a new future. God then draws a connection from a visual picture to an unperceived state to reposition his perception to a new place.

"Look up into the sky (Abraham had probably done this thousands of times) and count the stars if you can. (A visual picture). That's how many descendants you will have!" (New perceived reality, a new perception.) This new perception is cemented in Abraham's life by visualization of a known to a perceived unknow reality that he couldn't see. New perception was established by getting out of his comfort zone, visualizing something known and drawing a conclusion to help him see a new perception. Fourteen years later God again helped Abraham visualize his future by changing his name from Abram to Abraham. The name Abraham means "father of many nations." Every time he heard his new name being called it drew a visual image in his perception of the sky and how his descendant would be as many as the stars, constantly refocusing on this new perception until it was manifesting into the known world. That new perception was the driving point for his life until it manifested as a new reality with the birth of Isaac, his promised son by Sarah, when Abraham was 100 years old.

Viktor Frankl was a Jewish psychiatrist who spent three years during World War II living under unspeakable circumstances in several of the most notorious Nazi concentration camps. While imprisoned, Frankl realized he had one single freedom left: he had the power to determine his response to the horror unfolding around him.

And so he chose to imagine.

He imagined his wife and the prospect of seeing her again. He imagined himself teaching students after the war about the lessons he had learned.

Frankl survived and went on to chronicle his experiences and the wisdom he had drawn from them.

"A human being is a deciding being," he wrote in his 1946 book, *Man's Search for Meaning*, which sold more than 10 million copies. "Between stimulus and response there is a space. In that space is our power to choose our response. In our response lies our growth and our freedom."

But human perceptions, and their ramifications, are very real and potentially life changing.

I wasn't good in English class, which to me meant (my perception) I wasn't good in any aspect that had to do with English; grammar, spelling, sentence construction, reading, writing, etc. When I got up higher to a different vantage point (creative writing) I realized I may not be good in English but I was good in writing, (visualization of a new future) which led me to start reading, and for the first time I enjoyed reading. I started gathering books over the years and beginning to take time out of my day to read. My vantage point changed because I widened my horizons to new ideas and tried new things (got out of my perceived reality) and began visualizing what it would be like to write about things I loved.

This leads to the next thing to do to intentionally change your perception: you have to deal with your fear of failure.

Perception begins when the human brain receives data from the body's five senses. The mind then processes and applies meaning to the sensory information. Every life experience provides opportunities to learn something new, which can then be applied to create a better future. In today's society, failure has become something to fear, avoid, and therefore prevent at all costs. If success is *all* good and failure is *all* bad, then it seems as though we should do *everything we can* to remedy or prevent failure. A fear of failure can take a toll on a person's belief in their abilities and their motivation to pursue their goals. Many times, fear of failure is connected to our sense of self-worth or self-esteem. Fear of failure stems from a wrong belief about failure.

To effectively deal with "failure," we must address two

areas: first, your definition of failure and secondly, your perception of what it means to succeed. What is your definition of failure?

A research study in a New Zealand school investigated students' views about failure. The students were divided into overachievers and underachievers. In other words, students with high academic performance vs. students with low performance. The researchers found that students with high performance had different beliefs on failure than low performers.

Overachievers believe that failure is temporary, something that simply happens, and you must dust yourself off and keep moving. In contrast, underachievers believe that failure is permanent, that it stays with you forever. High achievers thought that failure says something about the task, while low performers felt it says something about themselves and their personality.

To fail is part of every journey and endeavor in life. We fail for a multitude of reasons; we aren't prepared, we didn't have enough knowledge, the option we chose didn't work out, the people were in the wrong position, etc. But we are only a failure if we didn't learn something from our last fail and we don't get up and improve upon our next try.

Kobe Bryant said, "Failure doesn't exist. It's a figment of your imagination. The point is the story continues. So if you fail on Monday, the only way it is a failure on Monday is if you decide to not progress from that, 'cause you know if I fail today I'm gonna learn something from that failure. I'm gonna try again on Tuesday, I'm gonna try again on Wednesday. The worst possible thing you could ever do is to stop and to not learn."

What if our definition of failure changed to mean failure is when we stop trying and learning how to accomplish something?

We would not be afraid to fail anymore because to fail is part of the journey of success. This leads us to the second thing.

To change your perception, you have to try new things that are uncomfortable for you to do. You feel vulnerable, with a sense of apprehension. In the past if you tried something and you weren't good at it, you interpreted it as this is an area you are not good at. This perception has closed many doors for you. You must challenge this interpretation; maybe it is something you aren't good at yet. But given the right amount of time, practice, knowledge, and energy you can be good at it.

By changing your perception, you reposition your reality. In life things will happen beyond our control. Once you reset your heart you can reposition your life by the way you interpret what has happened in those experiences. Realize that you get to shape your reality and will continue to see life through whatever perceptions you have created, so imagine and continue to go for new ideas!

CHAPTER 7

THINKING BIG

The washing David did of himself speaks of three areas: perception (which we just covered), thinking, and emotions. *Thinking* is working with our perceptions in different ways based on our needs and goals. The most common definition of thinking is that it is a logical process based on moving forward step by step to some sort of conclusion.

Perception is a very important part of thinking. Those who learn to manage perception become more powerful thinkers.

Thoughts can be defined as ideas, opinions and beliefs about ourselves and the world around us. Your thoughts affect your sense of reality, they can limit your abilities, they can change your perception, they can set you on the wrong course in life. But thoughts can also open us new pathways to life, they can enlarge your perception and they can release new abilities.

Throughout the past decade there has been many studies on the correlation of your thoughts and your brain. They have discovered that your thoughts can be used to change your brain. This process is called neural plasticity. In an article titled "Neural Plasticity: 4 Steps to Change Your Brain & Habits" by Dr. Kim and Dr, Hillary – June 21, 2010, they write:

"You can use your mind to change your brain and increase your happiness. *Neural pathways* are the biological result of your *habits of thinking, feeling and acting*. *Neural pathways* can be formed and strengthened into *new habits of thinking, feeling and acting*."

Even though your brain makes up only about 2 percent of your body's weight (about three pounds), it uses 20 to 30 percent of the calories you take in, as well as 20 percent or more of the oxygen and blood flow in your body. The brain uses its approximately 86 billion neurons, which fire 18 trillion times a second, to perceive and analyze incoming data; decide what, if anything, to do about it; and then execute your responses.

Our thoughts can continually keep us from repositioning our lives is our minds. We remember what we did, we remember how we did it, and sometimes we think that what has worked in the past will not work in the future.

Sometimes when we remember what we did and who it hurt, it haunts us and we cannot move forward. David's body and clothes are covered by dirt, his clothes with the smell of yesterday; the failures of the past, the loss of yesterday or the reminder of the previous season. He must wash the dirt and smell of yesterday off his life. You must wash off the dirt and smell of your past failings, missteps, falls, undervaluing and loss. Today we are prone to remember all the negative events, losses and undervaluing in our lives more than the positive ones. Our minds need to be washed from these thoughts from yesterday. **Paul uses the phrase "focusing all my energies on this one thing." He is relating the focus and energy it will take to reposition your thought life from the last season you just walked through.**

Paul understood how hard this is to do in real life, which is why he encouraged the Philippians church that had been through challenges to their faith, to wash their minds.

Philippians 3:13 NLT,

> *"No, dear brothers and sisters, I am still not all I should be, but I am focusing all my energies on this one thing: Forgetting the past and looking forward to what lies ahead."*

Once you have reset you must reposition our lives by putting out of your mind the thoughts of yesterday by washing them in the promise of God's Word (Ephesians 5:26 ESV "…that he might sanctify her, having cleansed her by the washing of water with the word"). God has ordained your life on this earth to do amazing things.

Ephesians 2:10 AMP,

"For we are God's own handiwork, recreated in Christ Jesus, that we may do those good works which God planned beforehand for us, taking paths which He prepared ahead of time, that we should walk in them living the good life which He prearranged and made ready for us to live."

You were recreated to do wonderful works that God planned out before you ever stepped into this world. You will fall short, misstep, mess up, suffer loss, and realize that you have changed for the better and life no longer fits. Resetting and Repositioning is how you move forward into the center of what God has planned for you to do on this earth. God has paths for you to walk that will bring fulfillment and purpose to your life. Others are awaiting your future steps. But like David, you have reset your heart and now you must reposition your life by repositioning your thought life.

There have been volumes of studies on the power of your thoughts. One of the recent is called "The Law of

Attraction." This concept builds on the ideas that thoughts create reality. According to this theory, we can attract what we want into our lives by focusing our thoughts and energy on them.

The Bible says it this way "For as he thinks in his heart, so is he." Proverbs 23:7 AMPC

"Before something can clearly be seen or perceived for what it is, thinking is already adding judgments and commentary, acting like a smoke screen," explains Peter Francis Dziuban in *Simply Notice: Clear Awareness is the Key to Happiness, Love and Freedom.*

Our thoughts influence our emotions and behaviors, and by changing our thoughts, we can change our lives. By focusing on positive thoughts, we can attract positive experiences, while negative thoughts can attract negative experiences. Studies have shown that positive thinking can improve mental health, reduce stress, and even boost physical well-being.

Science proves your thoughts influence your reality and shape your brain for better or worse. "Thoughts are real, tangible, measurable things — electrical impulses. Making sense of the world and what happens is the result of your individual brain's interpretation of the signals it receives as you go about your days interacting with your environment. It means that your brain assigns meaning to the electrical signals it receives." – Debbie Hampton, *The Best Brain Possible.*

A belief therefore is a thought that is repeated persistently, conscious or not, until it has been passed down as a part of your core beliefs or your personal belief system and mindset.

"Our minds aren't passive observers, simply perceiving reality as it is. Our minds actually change reality," said Alia Crum, an assistant professor of psychology and director of the Stanford Mind and Body Lab. She goes on to say "It's essential to recognize that mindset are central to health and behavior."

Mindsets are our mental attitudes or approaches to a particular situation or task. They are shaped by our thoughts and beliefs, and can impact our ability to adapt to change, solve problems, and achieve goals.

Mindset matters for more than health, of course. How people think about themselves – in particular, whether they think traits like intelligence are malleable – can have a powerful effect on their success in school and beyond.

For example: your significant other breaks up with you,

and suppose your thoughts are, "I will never find someone like him/her to love me again," this will most likely set into motion some very negative emotions like depression and then you will likely adopt behaviors consistent with depression such as staying in bed. But let's say that your thoughts are, "I'm glad it ended; he/she was just holding me back. Now I can move forward and find someone better!" Your thoughts determine your beliefs, actions, and ultimately your behavior. If you think these thoughts over and over and assign truth to them, they become beliefs. Beliefs create a cognitive lens through which you interpret the events of your world, and this lens serves as a selective filter through which you sift the environment for evidence that matches up with what you believe to be true. And then you get stuck in this cycle. This filtering system is called priming.

Priming means to use a substance to prepare something for use or action.

In Minnesota, my grandparents lived in an ancient cabin built out of logs; it was over 120 years old. They had a fresh spring that ran under the cabin with the most amazing tasting water. Inside the cabin they had this old hand pump and under the spout of this hand pump was a bucket with a little water in it. You would always leave a little water in the bucket because you would have to prime the pump by pouring water down the pump before you began to pump. Once you had poured water down the pump (primed it) you would begin hand pumping the pump and this fresh cold spring water would come flowing up from the spring into this bucket. Believe me, when you tasted that water it was like a little bit of heaven in your mouth.

Priming is like that in your thoughts, only this priming is the accumulation of thoughts formed into a belief. So when your brain is primed by a certain belief it shuts down competing neural networks, so you actually have a hard time seeing evidence to the contrary of what you already believe to be true. It's also why you are so convinced that your view of the world is the "truth." What most people don't realize is they are participating in creating their own version of the truth.

But the good news is, you can change your thoughts and reposition your life for the good things to come next. This will take time, consistent practice, and self-aware-ness of those negative thought cycles. Henry Ford said, "Whether you think you can or think you can't, you are right."

The first step is to **recognize the mind can be en-larged**. There is a story in the Bible of a man who was not in his right mind, but Jesus ministered to him and afterwards the text uses this phrase: "the man... sitting and clothed and in his right mind." Mark 5:15 BSB

This phrase right mind comes from a combination of two Greek words. Sozo means clear, safe, made whole, and Phroneo, which means the mind as a faculty of perceiving and judging, to fence or enclose, a confined boundary that can be enlarged and stretched. When we put these words together, we get this beautiful picture. Your thinking is the limiter, boundary maker, the enclosed restraints on your life. **This is where the idea of "limited beliefs" comes from. Your thoughts make up the boundary marker of your life today. Here is the good news.** As we allow our thoughts to be changed, our lives grow and become repositioned to a wide open, unlimited destination.

Your mind can shrink or grow. A single thought, when cultivated, grows over time into the empowering habit of thinking big that eventually takes over a person's psychology and propels them towards the achievement of the goals and objectives. A single thought that you intentionally hold on to and think over and over again and assign truth to becomes a belief. Almost everything that is man-made in this world started at some point as a single thought.

So what single thought do you need to grasp, hold on

to, and let play in your mind over and over again? Maybe it is the thought "Things change," that even though bad things happened to you growing up you can and will be different. Maybe it is the thought "I am unique," that even though you don't see much value in your life, you are very valuable and not replaceable. Maybe it is the thought, "The best parts of my life are ahead," that even though you have hit on some hard times you have the power and voice to say, "This is not how my story is going to end." Some have coined the idea of "a growth mindset." This is a belief that you can do what you set your mind to. Indeed, even as adults, the science shows that we can change our brains, learn new things, and develop new skills.

Author Michael Neill writes in *The Space Within: Finding Your Way Back Home*: "We live in a world of thought, but we think we live in a world of external experience."

The second step is to remember **everything starts small**. Rome wasn't built in a day; in fact, it started with a few hillside hamlets. Microsoft began as a backroom business. Howard Schultz is known for building the global brand Starbucks, but he actually started as an employee of the company. He joined the Seattle-based company in 1982 as the director of retail operations and marketing. Larry Page and Sergey Brin met at Stanford in the mid-

1990s and decided they wanted to start a company together. Two weeks later, the partners established Google's headquarters in Susan Wojcicki's 2,000 sq ft Menlo Park garage for $1,700 a month.

Everything starts out small. So it doesn't matter where you begin, where you are at right now because from small beginnings come great things.

In 1901, 21-year-old William S. Harley drew up plans to create a small engine to power a bicycle. Over the next two years, Harley and his childhood friend, Arthur Davidson, built their motor-bicycle out of their friend's 10 by 15-foot wooden shed in Milwaukee, Wisconsin. It was the equivalent of a garage because they didn't have cars.

They officially founded Harley-Davidson in 1903 and today it's the most well-known motorcycle brand in the world.

Harley-Davidson is a major US motorcycle manufacturer that sells its bikes worldwide through a network of more than 1,400 dealers. With annual revenue of $23.6 billion, it offers heavyweight cruiser and touring models, sport bikes, and dual models that can be used on- and off-road.

Sometimes we begin a course of action and find ourselves quitting because we didn't see the huge results we were expecting, never realizing that things were changing and given time they would grow to huge results. They say a plane that leaves Los Angeles heading for New York City but is only 3.5 degrees off will end up in Washington, DC instead of New York. Such a small change is barely noticeable at takeoff. The nose of the airplane moved just a few feet, but when magnified across the US, you end up hundreds of miles apart. DC is about 225 miles from New York City. The nose of the airplane moved just 3.5 degrees or about 86 inches. A very small shift in direction can lead to a very meaningful change in destination. A slight change in your thinking can guide your life to a very different destination. These 1% choices can make up the difference between who you are and who you will be.

By taking that one thought today and thinking about over and over again, "I am smart enough to figure things out," you create a new neuro pathway.

We do a lot of thinking daily, either consciously or otherwise. Experts estimate that between 50,000 and 80,000 thoughts go through our minds each day. That's about a thought every second, and that's even ignoring that we spend about a quarter or a third of the day sleeping. With so much thought consuming our day, isn't it necessary that we pay attention to them? *How much do you think about what you think about?*

Only 5% of those are new thoughts.

That means 95% of the time, we are repeating our thoughts over and over and over again.

Why is this important?

The third step is to realize your life gravitates in the direction of your most dominant thoughts.

We become what we think about most of the time.

The Roman emperor Marcus Aurelius wrote: "A man's life is what his thoughts make of it." What we think, what we perceive, and what we feel are the main components of our reality.

According to quantum physics, our thoughts are the source of reality. Everything that we see and experience is a product of thought energy.

It is not enough to begin to think a new thought; you must continue that thought intentionally. This process of intentionally and continually holding a thought is called meditation. Meditation is a part of creating new neural pathways that will change your brain and thought patterns. These neural pathways form and strengthen new habits of thinking. Joshua, who was thrust into the role of leading a nation, was told to "meditate on it (the book of instruction) day and night" and then he would prosper and succeed. Joshua would create new neural pathways through meditation, which would in turn create new habits of success.

As we discussed previously, that thought then becomes the foundation for a new belief to replace the old belief and reposition your life. You are the conductor of your own thoughts. Your dominant thoughts become the filter by which you act and behave, how you view the world around you.

A mind is more like a pile of millions of little rocks than a single big boulder. To change a mind, we need to carry thousands of little rocks from one pile to another, one at a time. This is because our brains don't know how to rewire a full belief in one big haul. New neuron paths aren't created that quickly. You might be able to get a tiny percent of someone's mind to rewire to a new belief in a given conversation, but minds change slowly so you have to be intentional in what you choose to hold in your thought patterns.

The fourth step is to **Let go of self-imposed limitations**. In order to truly thrive, you and I will have to let go of our self-imposed thought limitations. "They'll never hire me, I am not smart enough because I never finished college, this idea is too risky, I just not good at talking to others, it isn't my nature to be a leader."

Self-imposed thought limitations are thoughts or beliefs we have about ourselves that limit our potential. These thoughts/beliefs can be rooted in past fears, past experiences, or past social interactions. They can be thoughts about our abilities, our value, or our potential. These self-imposed thoughts can have significant impact on our lives. They can limit our ability to achieve our goals or pursue our dreams. They can prevent us from taking risks and trying new things. These thoughts have settled into areas of our lives in such a manner that we haven't realized that they are holding us back from repositioning our lives.

There is a story in the Bible that illustrates this point precisely.

The nation of Israel had waited almost 400 years to have their own land and place to settle in. God had promised that this land was flourishing beyond their anything they could imagine. Finally, the time came for them to step into this promise of God. They sent 12 mature leaders from all the tribes of Israel to see if what God said about the land was true. After 40 days they came back with a report and proof: two guys carried a cluster of grapes from the land on a pole between them. "When they reached the Valley of Eshkol, they cut off a branch bearing a single cluster of grapes. Two of them carried it on a pole between them, along with some pomegranates and figs." Numbers 13:23 NIV.

Then they began to give a report about what they saw, "We went into the land to which you sent us, and it does flow with milk and honey! Here is its fruit."

Then their conversation switched to self-imposed limitations.

"But the people who live there are powerful, and the cities are fortified and very large. We even saw descendants of Anak there."

They said, "The land we explored devours those living in it. All the people we saw there are of great size. We seemed like grasshoppers in our own eyes, and we looked the same to them."

What kept these leaders and the nation from what was a completion of a 400-year-old promise was self-imposed limitation that they put on themselves. It is clearly seen in the words "we seemed" – an interpretation of a particular situation, followed by a self-imposed limitation "grasshoppers in our own eyes." When you don't challenge these self-imposed thoughts, they become beliefs. Then you convince yourself everyone sees the same thing as you:

"and we looked the same to them."

These self-imposed beliefs must be identified and challenged as truth. First you must identify that self-imposed belief/thought, "If I have this conversation with this person it will end in a heated argument." Instead imagine how strong your relationship will become after having an open and honest conversation with this person.

If you want to overcome your self-imposed limitations, keep your mind open to new things, accept new ideas, and try different approaches. This will help you get out of your comfort zone and gain new experiences, which will help you grow as a person. As entrepreneur Richard Branson says in his book *Screw It, Let's Do It: Lessons in Life*, "If you opt for a safe life, you will never know what it's like to win."

The fifth step is to realize **everyone sees the same thing, but not everyone interprets what they see the same**.

In his book *Influence*, Dr. Robert Cialdini of Arizona State University relates the story of a jewelry store owner who was preparing to go on vacation and left tasks for her staff to perform. She had a line of jewelry that hadn't been selling well, and she wanted the price cut in half. In her haste, however, she left a note that was unclear. When she returned, she was delighted to find that every piece of the jewelry was gone. She was, however, shocked to find that her staff had doubled the price of the jewelry. The pieces that hadn't been selling went out the door immediately once the price was raised because it changed the way people thought about them.

Your thoughts and interpretations of circumstances directly influence your beliefs, and ultimately, your actions.

One of the tools to change the way you think is called *reframing*.

Research shows that what your body produces doesn't just depend on your subconscious brain, but also on your thoughts, feelings, and expectations. Knowing this, we can use thought reframing to help ease anxieties as well as potentially change the chemicals our brain is telling our bodies to create.

Simply put, reframing is changing how you see something and then expressing it differently. It's really a psychological paradigm shift that replaces your old way of thinking with a new and improved mindset. Reframing changes the way you see, think, and respond to situations.

Finding something to be grateful about in a challenging situation is an example of reframing. A big part of reframing is to realize thoughts are not facts, so they can be addressed and changed.

This is how it would work: instead of simply trying to talk yourself into a run (because you must exercise) on a cold, rainy morning when you'd rather hit snooze, imagine walking out and hearing the patter of the rain (it's okay, you're wearing a coat), feeling the cool breeze on your face, the sound of your footsteps hitting the pavement, your muscles working as you run, the taste of sweat on your lips, and how good and energizing it feels once you have finished. Envision the reward of a warm shower afterwards as you bask in exercise-induced endorphins. That feeling of accomplishment makes it much harder to hit snooze.

Reframing is noticing a thought, questioning the thought as fact, thinking of a positive outcome for that situation, and reframing the situation with a positive outcome.

By changing your thoughts, you reposition your life to a new destination, one that flows with the reset of your life and one that will take you to places you only dream of. "Now to Him who is able to [carry out His purpose and] do superabundantly more than all that we dare ask or **think**…" Ephesians 3:20 AMP

CHAPTER 8

EMOTIONALLY CONNECTED

The third area David washed himself in was his soul, in particular his emotions. Our emotions play a big part in how we respond to life's sudden changes. If our emotions are not repositioned, we will find ourselves acting and responding out of the past season instead of responding to this new season.

> *"The past has no power to stop you from being present now. Only your grievance about the past can do that. And what is a grievance? The baggage of old thought and emotion."*

> **- Eckhart Tolle**

Many things happen in our lives, and we tend to carry those thoughts and emotions with us throughout life. If we give those emotions from the past a home in our future, they will dictate our responses and actions in the future, keeping us tied to the past. You can find yourselves stuck in this cycle of feeling and responding from a past hurt or disappointment.

Emotions can direct our actions and cause us to behave

in a certain way. Emotions are a special class of motives that help us attend to and respond to important (usually external) situations and communicate our intentions to others. They can help you survive, grow, and connect with others. And they can guide your decisions, behaviors, and motivations.

Emotions can play a role in many aspects of life, including: growth and development, survival, higher levels of awareness, attention, motivation, learning and memory, decision making and problem solving, guiding behaviors, connection and attachment to others, overall well-being.

"Emotions matter because they typically dictate what will come next from us."

— **Chelsea Viñas,** licensed marriage and family therapist, owner of Therapize, a virtual private practice working with women in leadership on impostor syndrome, perfectionism, and trauma.

Research tells us of the importance of emotions.

A small 2014 study published by PubMed Central entitled "How emotions effect logical reasoning: evidence from experiments with mood-manipulated participants, spider phobics, and people with exam anxiety." Trusted Source suggested that emotions can influence how we think, make decisions and solve problems, especially with thinking tasks.

In a 2021 research review Trusted Source, researchers explained how emotions are a way humans evolved to address problems in a constantly changing world. They help us develop abilities to find food, water, shelter, sexual mates, support, and stay safe from dangers.

Emotions may also strongly affect our attention and memory, according to a 2017 review Trusted Source. When we have strong emotions or emotional events, we will often pay attention in more detail and remember things more clearly, for longer. This could be why traumatic events stick with us so vividly.

On June 27, 2014, 13-year-old Gavin England saved his grandfather from drowning when their prawning boat took on water and sank off the Saanich Peninsula on Vancouver Island (CTV, 2014). Gavin's grandfather Vern was not a strong swimmer, and though both were wearing life jackets, they would not have survived for long in the cold Pacific Ocean waters 300 meters from shore.

Gavin recounted the event, explaining how he suffered sharp cuts to his bare feet when climbing the embankment where he had dragged his grandfather. He attributed his ability to overcome the pain of the cuts to adrenalin. Upon finding an old truck with keys in the ignition, and despite the high emotions he was experiencing, he then had the wherewithal to learn to drive on the spot and make it up a three-kilometer hill to get help. Gavin explained that his knowledge of driving a dirt bike served him well: "I knew that clutch in meant drive." Vern described the young boy as "tenacious" and calm throughout the event. He was giving his grandfather words of encouragement as he pulled him to shore.

Emotions are a powerful force in our lives that can have significant impact on now and the future. Emotions help us make decisions and have a major impact on our mental and physical health.

Scientist Barbara Fredrickson has shown that positive emotions:

1. **Broaden** our perspective of the world (thus inspiring more creativity, wonder, and options)

2. **Build** over time, creating lasting emotional resilience and flourishing.

Dr. Fredrickson has spent years researching and publishing the physical and emotional benefits of positivity, including faster recovery from cardiovascular stress, better sleep, fewer colds, and a greater sense of overall happiness.

Emotions are constantly being generated — subconsciously or consciously — in response to memories of the past, experiences that were negative or positive, interactions with other or unsatisfied goals. We were designed to feel emotions. But what can cause us to dismiss emotions are "myths" we believe. We have all heard of myths like if you swallow gum it stays in your stomach for seven years, we only use 10% of our brains, cracking your knuckles causes arthritis, or sitting to close to the TV will cause you to go blind. This one hit home for us. My wife would say this to our 4-year-old son, and it wasn't until 1st grade that we realize he was sitting close to the TV because he couldn't see well and needed glasses.

The same thing can be said about the "myths" we believe about our emotions. Like "feelings are fickle" and "feelings are unreliable" and "don't trust your feelings."

Emotions are mentioned throughout the Bible and are a legitimate part of human life. God created humans with emotions because He has emotions and mankind is created in His image. Emotions are a good and gracious gift to every man and woman created in the image of God.

In the widely popular BBC show, *Sherlock*, intellectual prowess and the power of deduction are what make Holmes notable and iconic. However, in the episode "The Lying Detective," Holmes' landlady, Mrs. Hudson, insightfully points out that Sherlock is quite emotional, despite what is commonly thought, and behaves based on how he is feeling. Contrary to popular belief, he is not a calculating machine, but a human being with feelings. By the end of the episode, Holmes himself states, "It's not a pleasant thought, John, but I have this terrible feeling from time to time that we might all just be human" ("Sherlock Quotes," *Magical Quotes*). As poignantly depicted by the show, all people are emotional as part of their humanity.

Throughout the Bible, emotions are mentioned in great detail, like happiness, sadness, anger and genuine care for others. Emotions are a part of our everyday life.

There are things we do with our emotions that are unhealthy and can lead to other issues. Below I have listed a few of those unhealthy responses and the actions they can cause.

Suppress them – blow up at people or situations at the wrong time

Express all of them unfiltered – we become a raging forest fire of emotions

Become detached from them – we become an intellectual being with no emotional connections

Deny we have them – we bottle them up

Withdraw – we experience loneliness and depression

Many secondary problems stem from the fact that sometimes emotions are not a good indicator of reality and truth. Emotions can also have a huge negative impact on our lives. We have all heard of the term "emotional baggage." It is used to describe carrying our past negative experiences from life into future relationships, work, family, and life. These can affect the way we see ourselves, our physical well-being, our work production, our relationships with others and our ability to take calculated risks.

When we have been hurt by someone or some situation in the past, we will build up defense to protect ourselves from being hurt in the future. This can require a great deal of energy spent to keep the past alive. All of this can cause us to be stuck in the past season, even though we have reset our heart, repositioned our perceptive, and thought this one area can keep us from moving forward.

Emotions that are not repositioned from the previous season will affect the new season with wrong responses and actions in the new season.

Peter, a disciple of Jesus, is an example of just this fact. Peter was a fisherman who caught fish for a living; he owned a fishing business. Now Peter, a fisherman, becomes an assassin?

Then they came on him—grabbed him and roughed him up. One of those with Jesus pulled his sword and, taking a swing at the Chief Priest's servant, cut off his ear. Jesus said, "Put your sword back where it belongs. All who use swords are destroyed by swords." Matthew 26:51-52 MSG

When those with him saw what was happening, they said, "Master, shall we fight?" One of them took a swing at the Chief Priest's servant and cut off his right ear.

> *Jesus said, "Let them be. Even in this." Then, touching the servant's ear, he healed him.*
>
> **— Luke 22:50-51 MSG**

The account of this story in John 18 tells us the one with the sword is Peter. Peter, who is still emotional processing the previous season of events, carries those emotions into the next season and ends up maiming another person. How many times do we find ourselves doing something out of wrong emotions from the previous season? Maybe it is betrayal we suffered, or lies against us, or someone trying to destroy our reputation and we are still acting out from that previous season, not realizing in this new season we need to reposition our emotions so we can live in a new season. Peter misses the moment of the season he is in. He grabs his sword and almost assassinates this young man, thinking the whole time he is in the right response for this situation. It is only after Jesus corrects him and heals the young man's ear that Peter realizes his response is totally wrong for this season of life.

Can you relate? Are there moments you wish you would have responded differently?

So what can we do to reposition our emotions so our actions are in line with this new season we have stepped into?

When we experience emotions, we *feel* the experiences. When we become aroused, the sympathetic nervous system provides us with energy to respond to our environment. The liver puts extra sugar into the bloodstream, the heart pumps more blood, our pupils dilate to help us see better, respiration increases, and we begin to perspire to cool the body. The stress hormones *epinephrine* and *norepinephrine* are released. We experience these responses as arousal.

American pilot Captain "Sully" Sullenberger (Figure 11.1, "Captain Sullenberger and His Plane on the Hudson River") was 915 meters up in the air when the sudden loss of power in his airplane put his life, as well as the lives of 150 passengers and crew members, in his hands. Both of the engines on flight 1539 had shut down, and his options for a safe landing were limited.

Sully kept flying the plane and alerted the control tower to the situation: "This is Cactus 1539...hit birds. We lost thrust in both engines. We're turning back toward La Guardia."

When the tower gave him the compass setting and runway for a possible landing, Sullenberger's extensive experience allowed him to give a calm response: "I'm not sure if we can make any runway...Anything in New Jersey?"

Captain Sullenberger was not just any pilot in a crisis, but a former U.S. Air Force fighter pilot with 40 years of flight experience. He had served both as a flight instructor and the safety chairman for the Airline Pilots Association. Training had quickened his mental processes in assessing the threat, allowing him to maintain what tower operators later called an "eerie calm." He knew the capabilities of his plane.

When the tower suggested a runway in New Jersey, Sullenberger calmly replied: "We're unable. We may end up in the Hudson."

The last communication from Captain Sullenberger to the tower advised of the eventual outcome: "We're going to be in the Hudson."

He calmly set the plane down on the water. Passengers reported that the landing was like landing on a rough runway. The crew kept the passengers calm as women, children, and then the rest of the passengers were evacuated onto the rescue boats that had quickly arrived. Captain Sullenberger then calmly walked the aisle of the plane to be sure that everyone was out before joining the 150 other rescued survivors (Levin, 2009; National Transportation Safety Board, 2009).

Psychologists would call his responses *emotion regulation* — the ability to control and productively use one's emotions.

The first step in Repositioning your emotions is to realize your emotions are gauges, not a guide. You can read the gauge to measure the situation and regulate how you will respond emotionally to that situation. This means your emotions are meant to report a situation to you, not dictate your response. If you constantly create a narrative around your emotional experiences, the mind creates a smoke screen which conceals what is really taking place beneath the surface.

> *"When one door closes another door opens; but we so often look so long and so regretfully upon the closed door, that we do not see the ones which open for us."*

> **— Alexander Graham Bell**

You can choose how to respond emotionally to every situation. You are not a victim or helpless; you can interpret the situation and choose an appropriate emotional response. You can feel sad about the loss of a friendship, you can feel angry about being passed over for a promotion, you can feel happy about a friend coming to visit you, you can feel disgust about the something you see. These are all choices you make, but if you feel sad about the loss of a friendship and then believe it is because you are not good enough, the emotional response has gone from a gauge to a guide in your life.

Psychologist Robert Plutchick believed that humans can experience over 34,000 unique emotions but, ordinarily, they experience eight primary emotions. These primary emotions include **anger, fear, sadness, joy, disgust, sur-**

prise, trust, and anticipation. You make the choice if you will let emotions guide your life or give you an indication of that present situation.

The second step in all situations is to process what just happened and how we responded emotionally to the event.

Unprocessed emotional reactions to problems may themselves become new problems because of their negative impact on our overall emotional state and decision-making.

Emotions that are not processed will affect your immune system and keep it from working properly; **you might get sick more frequently and recover slowly**. Repressed emotions can also factor into mental health conditions, such as stress, anxiety, and depression. These issues often cause physical symptoms, including muscle tension and pain.

A 2017 study from Trusted Source suggested that when people practice acceptance (processing), they have better psychological well-being. When you accept things as they are, you're less likely to react first and think later. This may lead to you experience fewer negative emotions overall when you're stressed.

We may feel frustrated when we're stuck in traffic. We

may feel sad when we miss our loved ones. We can get angry when someone lets us down or does something to hurt us. But does our frustration in traffic lead us to flip people off and yell obscenities at them?

As adults, we are expected to manage our emotions in ways that are socially acceptable and help us navigate our lives.

Rapidly changing emotions can cause people to do and say things they later regret and be a sign to us that we are not handling things in the right way. They may damage relationships or hurt our credibility with others.

A very important skill in this step involves the ability to become aware of what we're feeling. Sometimes the feelings are buried deep within our souls. Journaling is a great way to get in touch with our emotions about a situation. How did that situation affect us, why did it affect us, and what was our response?

After noticing what you feel, the ability to name it can help you get control of what is happening. This helps you to regulate your emotional response to stay within healthy boundaries.

The Bible says it this way in Ephesians 4:26 NLT. "And don't sin by letting anger control you."

Notice what it does say, be angry; you will have a response of anger to some situation that happen to you in life. This is a normal, healthy emotion, not being suppressed. Where the line is crossed is when anger now guides your behavior and controls your response to that situation. If this has happened in the past, part of repositioning your emotions is to own that moment and change the way you think about that situation, which will change your response. This will help you begin to regulate your emotional responses to healthy boundaries.

You can help process emotional responses by asking yourself: what would you call the emotion you're feeling? Is it anger, sadness, disappointment, or resentment? What else is it? Did I respond the right way or did I go too far?

> *"Only by acceptance of the past can you alter it."*
>
> **— T.S. Eliot**

The third step is to release/forgive.

> *"The past was always there, lived inside of you, and it helped to make you who you were. But it had to be placed in perspective. The past could not dominate the future."*
>
> **— Barbara Taylor Bradford,**

Unexpected Blessings.

Emotional pain of the past can be held within the body if left unattended. A number of doctors have documented how emotions can cause a host of physical symptoms in the body.

Once we have processed these emotions, we must move forward into release/forgiveness.

> *"The act of forgiveness is the act of returning to present time. And that's why when one has become a forgiving person, and has managed to let go of the past, what they've really done is they've shifted their relationship with time."*

> **— Caroline Myss**

Almost everyone has experienced being wronged by someone. It could be a former co-worker, friend, or family member. But hanging on to those negative feelings can do great harm to your health.

Forgiveness entails forgiving oneself, forgiving others and receiving forgiveness from God. We are co-creators of our life's experience. Acknowledging this means no longer having to play victim to all that transpires in our lives.

When you learn to forgive, you are no longer trapped

by the past actions of others or yourself and your mistakes, so you can finally feel free.

Forgiveness means fully accepting that a negative event has occurred and relinquishing our negative feelings surrounding the circumstance. Research shows that forgiveness helps us experience better mental, emotional, and physical health. Forgiveness can be learned; those who have learned it well...

70% reported a decrease in their feelings of hurt

13% experienced reduced anger

27% experienced fewer physical complaints (for example, pain, gastrointestinal upset, dizziness, etc.)

The practice of forgiveness has also been linked to better immune function and a longer lifespan. Other studies have shown that forgiveness has more than just a metaphorical effect on the heart: it can actually lower our blood pressure and improve cardiovascular health as well.

Maybe you are reading these stats for the first time. So the question remains, if forgiveness is so beneficial for us why is it so hard to do?

Forgiveness is a multistep process. This may be why it is so hard to forgive. It requires a **decision** (intentionality), an **emotional choice**, a new **thought pattern,** and **ongoing persistence** in these three actions just mentioned.

The misconception is that forgiveness is a feeling. Forgiveness involves an intentional decision to let go of resentment and anger. Forgiveness doesn't mean forgetting or excusing the harm done to you. It also doesn't necessarily mean making up with the person who caused the harm. Forgiveness brings a kind of peace that allows you to reposition your emotions from past hurt and helps you go on with life.

The word forgive in the Bible has two Greek words that paint a beautiful picture of this intentional act.

The first word is charidzomai, from the Greek word *charis*, which means grace. It is used in Ephesians 4:32 NIV:

> *"Be kind and compassionate to one another, forgiving (charidzomai from charis) each other, just as in Christ God forgave (echarisato from charis) you."*

The idea of forgiveness here is cancelling a debt.

Luke 7:41-43 ESV

> *"'A certain moneylender had two debtors. One owed five hundred denarii, and the other*

fifty. When they could not pay, he cancelled (from charis, in some translations it is translated "forgave") the debt of both. Now which of them will love him more?' Simon answered, 'The one, I suppose, for whom he cancelled (from charis, in some translations it is translated "forgave") the larger debt. And he said to him, You have judged rightly.'"

The second word is the word *aphiemi,* which has the sense of "loose" or "let go."

The use of *aphiemi* is also found in 1 John 1:9 NIV:

If we confess our sins, he is faithful and just and will forgive (from aphiemi) us our sins and purify us from all unrighteousness.

When we forgive someone with the idea of aphiemi, we let something go. We don't bring it up again. We don't let it take over our hearts.

Some of the many translations of this word in the Greek is to send away, to abandon, to get rid of, to loose a ship from a place, to put out of the mind.

These ideas speak of an intentional decision to take this situation (you being hurt, you hurting someone else, or you coming up short) and putting it out of your mind. The only way to put it out of your mind is to then follow that decision with an emotional choice.

Emotional forgiveness is when you move away from those negative feelings and no longer dwell on the wrongdoing. Emotional forgiveness is much harder and takes longer, as it's common for those feelings to return on a regular basis. This often happens when you think about the offender, or something triggers the memory, or you still suffer from the adverse consequences of the action.

It is important to remember the difference between forgiveness and reconciliation. One common but mistaken belief is that forgiveness means letting the person who hurt you off the hook. Yet forgiveness is not the same as justice, nor does it require reconciliation. Emotional choice is an active process in which you make a conscious decision to let go of negative feelings whether the person deserves it or not. This choice frees you from experiencing that hurt over and over again.

Certain ancient Roman authorities were infamous for their sadistic manner, particularly when dealing with criminals. Most people are familiar with the gruesome and inhumane practice of crucifixion, but many consider another method of punishment even more shocking and appalling—one meted out by Roman tyrants most frequently upon murderers: They shackled the convicted killer to the dead body of his victim.

We gain some insight into this heinous practice from the poet Virgil, who described it in his *The Aeneid, Book 8,* starting on line 485:

The living and the dead at his command Were coupled, face to face, and hand to hand, Till, chok'd with stench, in loath'd embraces tied, The ling'ring wretches pin'd away and died.

Shackled to his victim, eye-to-eye, hand-to-hand, waist-to-waist, and foot-to-foot, the murderer—still very much alive—was forced to live out the remainder of his life directly bearing the weight and the putrefying stench of the dead body. In time, of course, the rotting flesh of the corpse would become rife with disease, infecting the killer and leading to a most horrible and grisly end.

This is a picture of what happens when we don't forgive emotionally as a choice.

**"To forgive is to set a prisoner free and
discover that the prisoner was you."**

— Lewis B. Smedes

It is not enough to make an intentional decision followed by an emotional choice to forgive. We must replace our thought pattern with a new one, one geared towards forgiveness.

Bob Enright, PhD, a psychologist at the University of Wisconsin, Madison, who pioneered the study of forgiveness three decades ago says, "True forgiveness goes a step further," he says, "offering something positive—empathy, compassion, understanding—toward the person who hurt you. That element makes forgiveness both a virtue and a powerful construct in positive psychology."

"Forgiveness involves the emotional reappraisal of the memory of a past wrongdoing," said Felipe De Brigard, a Duke neuroscientist and associate professor of philosophy. "When you forgive someone for a wrongdoing, you don't forget the event. But once you forgive, the memory doesn't hurt as much."

We choose to look through the lens of empathy at the other person or ourselves. A big way to do this is to ask God to help you see the situation through His eyes. When we see the situation through His eyes, empathy is realized in a way we didn't think was possible.

The last piece to this forgiveness puzzle is to realize this all is going to take time. The deeper the hurt, the longer the process of forgiveness.

This is captured in a story told in the Bible about hurt, unforgiveness, and something owed someone. The story in

Matthew 18 ends in verse 35. "That's what my heavenly Father will do to you if you refuse to forgive your brothers and sisters from the heart." NLT

The word heart here means the "center of your being." Forgiveness begins with your will, works its way through your emotions, into your thought patterns, and then eventually fills your hearts. This process can only be done through **ongoing persistence** to these three actions just mentioned above.

The fourth step in Repositioning your emotions is to talk back to your soul.

School teaches us all about the immense power of the mind, but it never teaches about the soul and the role it plays.

This is illustrated in the Bible in two consecutive chapters. Several times David is talking to his soul about what it is walking through emotionally.

Psalm 42:5, 6, 11 & 43:5 NIV

> *"Why, my soul, are you downcast? Why so disturbed within me? My soul is downcast within me; Why, my soul, are you downcast? Why so disturbed within me? Why, my soul, are you downcast? Why so disturbed within me?"*

From first glance it might appear David is schizophrenic, with two competing voices within himself. The first voice is an internal voice of his soul that is struggling with what he is walking through. We don't have an indication of what this conversation is, we only have an account of what he is saying to his soul. The second voice is his own voice out loud.

Notice David recognizes that his soul is struggling emotionally with something, and it is evident by the phrase he repeats three times; "Why so disturbed within me?" He actually talks back to his soul as if his soul can answer him and have a conversation with him. This lets us in on a huge skill in repositioning your soul. Don't let the internal conversation of your soul dictate the positioning of your perception, thinking and emotions.

David repositions his perception, thinking, and emotions in the response recorded in these verses, 5, 11 & 43:5:

> *"Put your hope in God, for I will yet praise him, my Savior and my God."*

And in verse 6 he actually draws his thinking into the conversation to fight this struggle in his soul to remain in the past.

"Therefore I will remember you (God) from the land of the Jordan, the heights of Hermon"

—from Mount Mizar

This is skill of talking to our soul needs to be developed. It requires three things to work effectually.

First, find a reposition perceptive (Abraham – my name means "Father of many nations;" I will let that be my perceptive, not barrenness), find a reposition thought (Abraham – It is so good to have the sound of children's voices in my tent and hear them call me "Dad").

Second begin to talk out loud those new perceptive and new thoughts. David said, "Put your hope in God, for I will yet praise him, my Savior and my God and I will remember you (God)." Third, find a place you feel comfortable and learn how to talk out loud. It can be very cathartic to your soul and whole being. And it causes the Repositioning of your emotions to stay steady in this new journey to a new destination.

CHAPTER 9

ATTITUDES AND BEHAVIORS

David resets his heart, then he repositions his life. David does this repositioning by washing his perception, thoughts and emotions from the old to the new and then covers himself with the anointing of God's grace for this repositioning.

Then David next changes his clothes, a sign that he is not the same man anymore. David has now Reclothed his life!

In our world, clothing matters. There is a saying that has been around for hundreds of years now. "Clothes make the person." We care about clothing because it reflects who we are. Clothing makes a statement about ourselves. Clothes reflect your profession, your social status, your values, and your beliefs.

Changing one's clothes is symbolic of changing his attitudes and behaviors. David needs to Reclothe his attitudes with ones that will be in sync with a Reset, Repositioned life.

The Bible picks up on this idea in Ephesians 4:23-24 NLT:

"Instead, let the Spirit renew your thoughts and attitudes. Put on your new nature, created to be like God—truly righteous and holy."

In the previous verse (22) it uses this analogy "to put off your old self." The phrase "put off" is used for setting aside clothing. It is often translated "put away" in the New Testament. We are to take off and put away our old self, meaning the way we used to live life. And then we put on "new attitudes."

The **NRSV** translation says it this way: "...**and to clothe yourselves with the new self, created according to the likeness of God in true righteousness and holiness.**"

We need new attitudes that partner with repositioned perception, thinking, and emotions.

Viktor Frankl spent a total of three years in four concentration camps: Theresienstadt, Auschwitz, Kaufering III, and Türkheim. He lost his father in the Terezín Ghetto, his brother and mother at Auschwitz, and his wife in the Bergen-Belsen concentration camp. Frankl and his fellow prisoners had everything stripped from them. Their families, friends, jobs, health, possessions and even their names. Most men in the concentration camp grew to believe that the real opportunities of life had passed them by.

While working in a camp hospital, Frankl noticed the death rate spiked the week between Christmas and New Year's in 1944.

"The death rate in the week between Christmas, 1944, and New Year's, 1945, increased in camp beyond all previous experience. In his opinion, the explanation for this increase did not lie in the harder working conditions or the deterioration of our food supplies or a change of weather or new epidemics. It was simply that the majority of the prisoners had lived in the naïve hope that they would be home again by Christmas. As the time drew near and there was no encouraging news, the prisoners lost courage and disappointment overcame them." Viktor Frankl, *Man's Search for Meaning,* Beacon Press, 1947.

Yet in reality, there was an opportunity and a challenge. One could make a victory of those experiences, turning life into an inner triumph, or one could ignore the challenge, as did a majority of the prisoners.

Frankl and his fellow prisoners had everything taken from them but there was one thing that remained truly their own. Namely, we get to choose how to react to any given thought, emotion, or set of circumstances.

"Everything can be taken from a man but one thing: the last of the human freedoms—to choose one's attitude in any given set of circumstances, to choose one's own way."

According to Viktor Frankl, although people are not always free to choose the conditions in which they find themselves, they are always free to choose their *attitude* towards these conditions and, thus, are always free to find their lives meaningful.

"Even though conditions such as lack of sleep, insufficient food and various mental stresses may suggest that the inmates were bound to react in certain ways, in the final analysis, it becomes clear that the sort of person the prisoner became was the result of an inner-decision and not the result of camp influences alone. Fundamentally then, any man can, under such circumstances, decide what shall become of him – mentally and spiritually." Viktor Frankl, *Man's Search for Meaning,* Beacon Press, 1947.

Let me say that again "You get to choose your attitude in every given set of circumstances." So choose wisely.

Your Attitude determines the Altitude of your life. Your life will never rise above your attitude. Your life will never reach its full potential (what you were created to be) if your attitude remains the same.

When I was a kid one of the things we loved to do on a hot, windy day was go to the beach and fly kites. In Santa Barbara we have several beaches, all with different attributes that make them amazing. If you want to play volleyball, East Beach is the best; if you want to hang out and rest, there is a beach by the City College that is cozy and restful. If you are looking to surf, there are a couple of beaches where the waves can be pretty good at certain times. But if you want to fly a kite, the beach that was great for doing this was a beach called Henry's Beach. The beach was nestled in this cove surrounded by cliffs. You would pull into the parking lot, this wide-open space leading down to the beach. As you parked your car and headed toward the beach, there was an area about 100 yards long by about 30 yards wide. The waves would be rolling in in front of you, with the sand beckoning you to come. As you walked towards the beach, on either side of this wide-open space were cliffs that protected the beach. The cliffs would run to the left and right of this space parallel to the water. Once you got to sand, you could go right or left onto the beach. The beach was 30 yards wide, with the water as a boundary on one side and this towering cliff as a boundary on the other side. The cliff was about 40-50 feet high and ran the length of the beach. The beach sand looked like it ran endlessly toward the right as far as your eye could see. We would wander down about ½ mile to where it was less crowded and set down our towels. The wind was blowing lightly on the beach, enough to cool the sun's rays. We would get out our kites, the old-fashioned type, in the shape of a diamond with a homemade tail on the end. We would attach the string, good old fashioned fishing wire. If we tried to fly the kite on the beach the kite would just flounder, because the wind on the beach level was not strong enough to get kite up high in the air. The wind would blow sand in your eyes as you were lying on your towel and cool you off if the temperature rose, but was not enough wind to fly your kite. It was just enough wind to cause the kite to move back and forth but not enough wind to get high in the air. <u>So through experience we came up with a way to get the kite the altitude it needed to perform the way it was created</u>. One of us, my brother or a friend, would hold it as high in the air as we could, then the other would take off running as fast as he could down the beach. As we ran, we would let out the fishing wire a little at a time. The resistance we were creating by pulling the kite against the wind combined with giving it just the right amount of line caused the kite to slowly rise. Too much line and the kite would quickly fall, not enough and the kite would struggle and eventually dive bomb into the sand, sometimes separating the kite. We would run with this delicately balanced line and resistance and learned from countless times of watching the kite dive bomb or flounder. When we were almost ready to drop from the tiredness of running, we would watch the kite begin to rise on its own. As it rose to the heights of the cliffs, as it climbed to that magical place, the wind across the tops of the cliffs would take the kites and hold them in the air. They would literally look like they were suspended in the air. The kite had risen to the place where it was created to soar. It reached the altitude where the wind was not an adversity keeping it down but an aid in causing it to soar. <u>The kite was at the altitude where it was designed to function best, to do what it was created to do</u>. We could set the kite in the ground and anchor it; it would stay the rest of the day, as long as the wind didn't die down. We could then go body surfing, relax, eat, play Frisbee or football, and the kite would just do its thing.

In this chapter and the next, we will gain understanding of how to develop the right attitudes to achieve the altitude you need to maintain to live in this new Reset and Repositioned life.

Attitude is one of the most powerful things you possess.

A person's mental attitude has an almost unbelievable effect on his powers, both physical and psychological. The British psychiatrist, J.A. Hadfield, gives a striking illustration of this fact in his booklet, The Psychology of Power. "I asked three people," he wrote, "to submit themselves to test the effect of mental suggestion on their strength, which was measured by gripping a dynamometer." They were to grip the dynamometer with all their strength under three different sets of conditions. First he tested them under normal conditions. The average grip was 101 pounds. Then he tested them after he had hypnotized them and told them that they were very weak. Their average grip this time was only 29 pounds! In the third test Dr. Hadfield told them under hypnosis that they were very strong. The average grip jumped to 142 pounds.

Psychologists define attitudes as a learned tendency to evaluate things in a certain way.

Attitudes are formed/learned by experiences, social factors, conditioning, and observation. Learned is the key word here. If they are learned, they can be changed and cultivated by the right influences.

The word cultivate means *to bestow attention, care, and labor upon, with a view to valuable returns; to direct special attention to; to devote time and thought to; to im-*

prove by labor, care, or study; to refine; to care for while growing; apply oneself to improving or developing (one's mind or manners.

Cultivating requires a <u>decision,</u> a <u>fresh vision,</u> <u>knowledge,</u> <u>hard work,</u> and <u>followthrough.</u>

The writer, Paul, of the letter to the Philippians gives us clarity on what Attitudes we should cultivate in our lives.

Philippians 2:5 NASB:

> *Have this attitude in yourselves which was also in Christ Jesus.*

This word, attitude, is the Greek word phren (frane), which means to have an opinion, to direct one's mind to a thing; it implies moral reflection.

Paul chose the word "Have," which implies our responsibility to let it happen. Our choice to accept or change (cultivate) the right attitude.

It is easy to say, "Well, things in the city of Philippi, to the people Paul is writing to, are easier than my situation." But this couldn't be farther from the truth.

Philippi was not an easy place to live out your faith. It was a Roman colony established by those loyal to Rome, who held to the belief that Rome and the belief system of

Rome were the only way to live. They would persecute all those with other beliefs; this is what happened to Paul when he went to Philippi in Acts 16.

Because of this hostility against Christ-followers, it was easy to focus on self, develop wrong attitudes, and live out their faith in solitude. Paul was reminding them that what they possessed could change the world, as long as it was joined with the right attitudes.

The first attitude we need to cultivate in this Reset and Repositioned life is the Attitude of Gratitude.

The word gratitude is derived from the Latin word *gratia*, which means grace, graciousness, or gratefulness.

Gratitude - *The state of being grateful; warm and friendly feeling toward a benefactor; kindness awakened by a favor received; thankfulness.*

Thankfulness - *Impressed with a sense of kindness received, and ready to acknowledge it.*

Gratitude/Thankfulness is an attitude that is disappearing fast in our present society. When you held the door open for someone else it used to be common practice to say, "Thank you." Today people feel a sense of entitlement: "I deserve this", "I earned this." This new attitude flies in the face of thankfulness; it makes it all about you.

This entitlement has led to other destructive attitudes that are presently abounding around us. It is so vital we do cultivate "thankfulness" in our lives. Studies have shown that feeling thankful can **improve sleep, mood, and immunity**. Gratitude can decrease depression, anxiety, difficulties with chronic pain, and risk of disease. In positive psychology research, gratitude is strongly and consistently associated with greater happiness. Gratitude helps people feel more positive emotions, relish good experiences, improve their health, deal with adversity, and build strong relationships.

Two psychologists, Dr. Robert A. Emmons of the University of California, Davis, and Dr. Michael E. Mc-Cullough of the University of Miami, have done much of the research on gratitude. In one study, they asked all participants to write a few sentences each week, focusing on particular topics.

One group wrote about things they were grateful for that had occurred during the week. A second group wrote about daily irritations or things that had displeased them, and the third wrote about events that had affected them (with no emphasis on them being positive or negative). After 10 weeks, those who wrote about gratitude were more optimistic and felt better about their lives. Surprisingly, they also exercised more and had fewer visits to physicians than those who focused on sources of aggravation. These are just of the few scientific reason that the attitude of Gratitude will change your life for the better.

In the Bible there is a story that reveals to us the greatest impact that cultivating Gratitude will have on our lives.

Luke 17:11-19 KJV

> *And it came to pass, as he went to Jerusalem, that he passed through the midst of Samaria and Galilee. And as he entered into a certain village, there met him ten men that were lepers, which stood afar off. And they lifted up their voices, and said, Jesus, Master, have mercy on us. And when he saw them, he said, unto them, Go shew yourselves unto the priests. And it came to pass that, as they went, they were cleansed. And one of them, when he saw that he was healed, turned back, and with a loud voice glorified God, And he fell down on his face at his feet, giving him thanks: and he was a Samaritan. And Jesus answering said, Were not there ten cleansed? But where are the nine? There are not found that returned to give glory to God, save this stranger. And he said unto him, Arise, go thy way: thy faith hath made thee whole."*

Let us look at some things in this story that will help us cultivate Gratitude in our lives. This story also shows us the powerful impact gratitude can have upon our lives.

Jesus was traveling between towns. Coming to a particular village Jesus was drawn to the shouts of 10 men in a desperate situation. Leprosy was not just a horrible disease but also a social death sentence. "They were required to live outside the camp or the city. This disease was regarded as an awful punishment from the Lord. They had to warn passers-by to keep away from them by calling out 'Unclean! Unclean!' nor could they speak to anyone, or receive or return a salutation, since in the East this involves an embrace."(*Easton Bible Dictionary*)

"It gradually spreads, its internal disfigurement, its dissolution little by little of the whole body, of that which corrupts, degrades and defiles man's inner nature, and renders him unmeet to enter the presence of a pure and holy God." (*Maclear's Handbook O.T.*)

This disease robbed them of any social life and community, drained them of all financial life, slowly isolated them from emotional connection as they could not touch anyone, and disconnected them from connection to the practice of their religion in community.

They cried out for mercy, not healing. Mercy here means to show kindness and concern for someone in serious need. They asked for compassion for their state, not healing.

What happened next is so important for us to pause and reflect on. They cried out to Jesus and it says Jesus saw them. This word means to perceive, to visit. When we are walking through a tough time, we can feel like we are alone, we can feel like God doesn't really see us. This tells us when we cry out to God in this tough season, God does see us and if He sees us, He will respond to us in His timing.

Jesus told them to "show themselves to the priest." This was the only way someone excommunicated by leprosy could get back into society. The priest of God had to be involved in the cleansing process to allow the individual back into society by approving the person as being cleansed.

Here is another point to pause and reflect on: they were quite a far walking distance from the city to show themselves to the priest. One of the first things leprosy destroys is your fingers and toes. So they had to begin to walk toward their future in a lot of pain. We don't know how long this journey was or how long they had to walk in pain. Sometimes the way out of your situation is not a miracle but to walk out of your pain, feeling the effects of your decision to walk out of it every step you take. Keep walking!

Each step was more painful than the first, but somewhere along the journey the pain suddenly stopped. They looked down and realized the disease was completely gone.

What happened next is a key for us.

Nine continued their journey to get approval from the priest so they could enter back into society and see their loved ones. But one of them did something unexpected. *"One of them, when he realized that he was healed, turned around and came back, shouting his gratitude, glorifying God."*

Remember, attitudes are cultivated through life choices and internal disciplines. So that makes this all the more amazing. This man returned to give thanks, "shouting his gratitude." This man, in the midst of one of life's most horrible diseases and outcast to society, painfully dying a little every day, developed an attitude of Gratitude/Thankfulness. Let that sink in: your life may be extremely hard, you may be going through the fight of your life, everyone you love may have deserted you, society may no longer embrace you, and you may feel like you are just biding your time till death finally takes over. But you do not have to be a victim of your circumstances! In the midst of all that is going on, you can choose to develop an attitude of Gratitude/Thankfulness. Cultivate… when did this man have the time or frame of mind to cultivate Gratitude? What did this man have to be thankful for? What could he possibly find in his life to give thanks for? This man was a Samaritan, who grew up being hated by the Jews and wasn't allowed into their places of worship. This man was rejected twice, first by the Jews, then by his own people. He wasn't the most likely person to show Gratitude to God. Yet this man, in the midst of great rejection, cultivated a thankful attitude. When others got bitter and blamed God, he cultivated a thankful attitude. It was that gratitude that motivated him to travel all the way back, putting his life on hold, delaying his restoration to society and his loved ones. All because of a thankfulness attitude. Life is a journey not a sprint; how your travel through life is up to you; you are the determining factor, not circumstances. Think about this one man's journey back. What was motivating his life to endure the journey back?

He got what he wanted; this dreaded disease was gone, he now had the ability to go back to society and his love ones.

Yet this man could not go forward until he gave thanks for what he had received, no matter what it cost. His journey back involved energy, time, and reality that he had nothing more to gain for himself.

However, his journey was not for others but for himself; he needed to give thanks. This attitude was cultivated in his life and his life was entwined in this attitude.

Entertaining a healthy outlook of gratitude leaves very little or no room for discontent and resentment. As a great sage named Fred Smith once said, "I find that it is hard to be depressed and grateful at the same time. Therefore, I discipline my mind to be thankful for the blessings of the present."

He kneeled at Jesus' feet, so grateful. He couldn't thank him enough—and he was a Samaritan.

This Samaritan chose how he would live his life; he took back the ownership of his life. He decided life's circumstances would not influence how he would live. You can begin to take back ownership of your life from that feeling of helplessness by choosing how you will respond to what happens in life. It was a daily decision that he needed to maintain.

Here is the reward of developing a grateful attitude.

Luke 17:19 KJV:

And he said unto him, Arise, go thy way: thy
faith hath made thee whole.

It brought wholeness back to his life; it just didn't heal of the disease but restored what the disease had taken from him. **When you walk in an attitude of Gratitude, that attitude opens up the restorative power to bring back what was lost.**

> *"God gave you a gift of 86,400 seconds to-*
> *day. Have you used one to say "thank you?"*

— William A. Ward

So how do you begin to take back ownership of your life? How can you cultivate an attitude of Thankfulness?

Let's Look at Three Steps to Cultivating the Attitude of Gratitude in Your Life.

You start by changing what you will focus on. Focus is an amazing tool; you literally blur out certain things/facts in order to clearly see other things. Focus is a central point of attention (Dicitonary.com); adjustment for distinct vision; the area that may be seen distinctly or resolved into a clear image.

You may at one time have looked at a 3D picture. You

have to blur your focus for what is perceived, in order to see what is not clearly seen. What is clearly before you is not really the picture but the true picture is hidden within the appeared picture. If you are like me, the hardest thing to do with those pictures is to blur my focus to what is in front of me; it takes great effort. I have to constantly blur because the natural tendency of my eyes are to focus on what is before me. So as I start to blur my eyes, they refocus again on what is before me. After several times of this struggle, finally my eyes blur to what is before me and see the picture within the picture. This is true in life; what you see is many times not the picture you should be focusing on. Sometimes you are in a situation that appears so real, you cannot see anything but the circumstances. So you must continually fight to blur your eyes to what is before them and see what is not so clearly evident. Make a decision today that you will cultivate an attitude of gratitude, by beginning to change your focus.

Thessalonians 5:18 NIV tells us to "Give thanks in all circumstances, for this is God's will for you in Christ Jesus."

Notice what it says in all circumstances, not for all circumstances. This is a key to cultivating the attitude of gratitude.

What you focus on will have profound effects on your life. Every day your vision is bombarded by images, images that want to be the reality of your life. You decide whether that image or another will become your focus. Your job is about to have layoffs. If you focus on the reality that you haven't been there that long, then you will begin to think that you will be the first to go and your life becomes filled with anxiety. Or you focus on the fact that God gave you that job, and if it goes away God will provide you another, so you are filled with a sense of peace about your future.

Focus is adjusting your vision to what you will see clearly. So you will have to look to find some positive aspect in the middle of your present situation.

Focus is about getting the right picture to form (some positive image in the midst of what is going on) the right attitude, but you must hold on to that image even when circumstances are showing you a contrary image. This leads to Step 2.

Step 2 is meditation on that new image.

Meditation is how you hold on to your focus.

Meditation means to focus one's thoughts on, to dwell on anything in thought; to contemplate; to turn or revolve any subject in the mind; to keep the mind fixed upon.

Meditation is the discipline to keep your mind focused on that positive image you found to be grateful for in spite of situations, circumstances, and life happening. It is not easy; life can be very convincing, but if you keep the image you obtained through focus and then think about it, revolving it in your mind, fixing your thought energy on that which you can be thankful for, your life will cultivate a grateful attitude. Meditation implies a discipline of putting your mind on that positive image and pulling it back to that image as other images try to become your focus. You cannot control life, no matter how hard you try, but you can control your response to life.

This brings us to the 3rd step.

The 3rd Step is to Refocus.

Throughout the day, you will have moments of refocusing, things that will help you cultivate a Grateful attitude. They will be ever so slight, and many times you will miss them unless you realize what to do with them. When they come, they give you an opportunity to refocus from the things around you to a grateful attitude.

My wife was having a busy day loaded with struggles and unfulfilled dreams, the weight of which was pulling heavy on her soul. As evening approached, the day had taken its toll on her soul and affected her attitude of gratefulness. Then our little guy (not so little now), Tytus, came over and snuggled into my wife and said to her, "Mom, I love you, will you marry me?" That "refocus moment" allowed her to take her mind off of everything else and put it on that moment, helping her maintain a Grateful attitude.

On September 13, 2004, Oprah Winfrey celebrated her 19th season on TV. She celebrated by giving away a new car to every person in her audience that day. The 276 audience members were selected because friends or family had written about their need for a new car. One couple had 400,000 miles on their two vehicles. One mom wrote in that her son drove a car that looked like it had been in a gunfight. Oprah began by calling 11 people out of the audience onto the stage. She gave each of them a brand-new Pontiac G6. Then she distributed a gift box to everyone in the audience. She told them that one of them contained the keys to a 12th new car. But when the audience opened the boxes, each one had a set of keys in it. Oprah started jumping up and down yelling: "Everybody gets a car! Everybody gets a car!" There was pandemonium on the set as everyone yelled and hugged each other. Then they went to the parking lot of Harpo Studios to see their cars, all decorated with giant red bows. But one writer commented, "All is not well in Oprah Land. Now the people who received the new cars are complaining. Even though the local taxes and licensing fees were covered as a part of the gift, the IRS is going to take a sizable bite out of their pocket, because the $28,000, which is the value of the car, will be added to their income for this year. Their state income tax will also go up. Some of the winners thought that all this should have been taken into account and they should have been given the cash to cover these expenses as well."

> *"As we express our gratitude, we must never forget that the highest appreciation is not to utter words, but to live by them."*
>
> **— John Fitzgerald Kennedy**

CHAPTER 10

A CAN-DO ATTITUDE

The second attitude we need to cultivate in this Reset and Repositioned life is a Can-Do attitude.

A can-do attitude is a positive mindset that helps you achieve anything you want to. Having a can-do attitude means you take a proactive approach to all situations, believing you can tackle any challenges and face any difficulties that occur in life. When you have a can-do attitude, no problem is too big to solve.

A can-do attitude is learning to be positive when faced with any situation. This is a learned attitude; it can be developed by transforming our negative thoughts into positive thoughts. This can be a tricky thing to do, as many of us flow between negative thinking patterns and positive thinking patterns and back and forth in everyday life without consciously being aware we have shifted.

Long ago in a deep mountain valley verdant with growth and watered by a crystalline river, there lived a tribe. They prospered and grew until the grass was graz away, the game hunted into extinction, and the river ran dry. A group of young pioneer heroes rose up to say, "We have heard of a wider valley and deeper rivers over the mountains where no one has gone. Let us be up and going."

They made their way to the deeper valley with the wider stream, and it was as they had heard. They returned with their report to the tribal council. There was, however, a council called "The Old Men Who Know." They responded that there could be no such place, and even if there were, the tribe could never make the journey.

The young heroes struggled until most of the tribe died. Finally they made their way over the mountain to the land of the future. There they grew and prospered once again. Finally, the day came when the grass in the new valley had been grazed down and the water ran low. A new group of young pioneer heroes arose and claimed that beyond the next mountain there was an even larger valley with more grass and great herds of game.

But the strangest thing had happened. The original young pioneer heroes had in one generation become "The Old Men Who Know." Their positive can-do attitude shifted to a negative "We're not able" attitude.

A can-do attitude is characterized by a positive outlook on life and a belief that you can overcome challenges and achieve your goals. The benefits of a can-do attitude are numerous. Research has shown that people with a positive mindset have better mental health outcomes, including lower rates of depression and anxiety. They also tend to have better physical health, with lower rates of heart disease and stroke (University of California study).

A can-do attitude helps you develop resiliency and take on the challenges presented to you in life, whether big or small. Being resilient is key to riding out the ups and downs of life.

The key to a can-do attitude is a positive outlook on life and the belief that you can overcome any challenges.

Remember that behavior changes biology. Positive gestures benefit you by releasing oxytocin, a hormone that helps connect people. Some people call it the love hormone.

You'll also benefit the person on the other end of the gesture.

A person's mental attitude has an almost unbelievable effect on his powers, both physical and psychological. The British psychiatrist, J.A. Hadfield, gives a striking illustration of this fact in his booklet, The Psychology of Power. "I asked three people," he wrote, "to submit themselves to test the effect of mental suggestion on their strength, which was measured by gripping a dynamometer." They were to grip the dynamometer with all their strength under three different sets of conditions. First he tested them under normal conditions. The average grip was 101 pounds. Then he tested them after he had hypnotized them and told them that they were very weak. Their average grip this time was only 29 pounds! In the third test Dr. Hadfield told them under hypnosis that they were very strong. The average grip jumped to 142 pounds.

What is a Positive Attitude? It is an attitude characterized by optimism, enthusiasm, and a focus on the bright side of situations. A positive attitude can lead to increased motivation, perseverance, and problem-solving abilities, enabling individuals to provide exceptional experiences consistently. It also helps foster a healthy work environment, promoting collaboration and teamwork.

> *"If you have a positive attitude and constantly strive to give your best effort, eventually you will overcome your immediate problems and find you are ready for greater challenges"*

— Pat Riley

David had made some bad choices that led to him Resetting and Repositioning his life. But he recovered and moved forward because he developed a can-do attitude.

Whatever David's decisions produced in the previous season   was not permanent; he could plant a new crop for a new season to reap a new harvest. God had something amazing in his next season! So many struggle with this today; they find it hard to believe that they can move through this Reset/Reposition and see something great in their next season. Here is a big reason why: we tend to remember negative experiences better than positive experiences.

Many studies suggest that we are more likely to remember negative experiences over positive experiences, and according to Laura Carstensen, a psychology professor at Stanford University, in general, we tend to *notice* the negative more than the positive.

Carstensen said one school of thought believes that our attention to negative events has adaptive value. She said there's a lot of information to be learned in difficult or dangerous situations, and that our brains can apply that knowledge when a similar situation presents itself in the future.

In every situation we are presented with two different opposing views of that situation. One is a positive outcome and the other a negative outcome.

This happened in the nation of Israel many years ago. The story is found in Numbers 13-14. The back story is that after hundreds of years, Israel was finally let go from slavery in the nation of Egypt. They began to journey toward a land that was promised 400 years earlier to their great-great grandfather Abraham. The nation of Egypt then chased after them to kill them or bring them back. By God's providence, the nation of Israel was saved in a dramatic way as they crossed over the Red Sea toward the Promised Land and the army of Egypt was destroyed in the Red Sea.

Israel journeyed a little farther and stood by the Jordan River, ready to cross into the land God promised them. The story picks up with them sending out 12 leaders (spies), one leader from each of the 12 tribes. These were experiences, highly respected, mature and chosen by their tribe to be one of their leaders. They were told to check out the land to see what God had promised them 400 years earlier was true, and to bring back fruit as proof of God's faithfulness to them.

Here is where we will begin.

Numbers 13:25-27 NLT

> *After exploring the land for forty days, the men returned to Moses, Aaron, and the whole community of Israel at Kadesh in the wilderness of Paran. They reported to the whole*

community what they had seen and showed them the fruit they had taken from the land. This was their report to Moses: "We entered the land you sent us to explore, and it is indeed a bountiful country—a land flowing with milk and honey. Here is the kind of fruit it produces.

From this part of the story, it seems that everything is just as God said. But it quickly becomes about another viewpoint, and the first viewpoint is lost and devalued as even a part of the story.

Numbers 13:28, 31-33 NLT

But the people living there are powerful, and their towns are large and fortified. We even saw giants there, the descendants of Anak!

"We can't go up against them! They are stronger than we are!"... "The land we traveled through and explored will devour anyone who goes to live there. All the people we saw were huge. We even saw giants there, the descendants of Anak. Next to them we felt like grasshoppers, and that's what they thought, too!"

Ten of these leaders only saw the obstacles and negative issues. They lost sight of the promise and the one who made the promise. When you allow a negative story to be told in your mind, your mind will grasp that story and run it on repeat. The result of that repeated story is a negative attitude that produces a magnification of the facts to a place of a distorted view of life.

These fearless, experienced, and mature leaders were now the originators of a negative story being told. These leaders ended the story by saying "they thought we were grasshoppers too."

Two of the leaders told another story, one filled with promise, one filled with positivity and a "can-do" attitude.

Numbers 14:6-7, 9 NLT

> *Two of the men who had explored the land, Joshua son of Nun and Caleb son of Jephunneh, ... They said to all the people of Israel, "The land we traveled through and explored is a wonderful land! ...don't be afraid of the people of the land. They are only helpless prey to us! They have no protection, but the LORD is with us! Don't be afraid of them!"*

In every circumstance we are presented with two different opposing views of that circumstance. One is a positive outcome and the other a negative outcome.

Here is the takeaway: to move into this Reset and Reposition life you must not allow the negative challenges of the past season to influence and color this new season. The problems, challenges, losses, mistakes and undervaluing experiences that mark the previous season are not indicators of this new season. This new season is one with possibilities! Sure, it will have its own set of challenges, but your Reset heart and Reposition perception, thinking, and emotions will take you to a different destination because you set yourself up for a bright future. So don't take any of the previous season with you.

The nation of Israel had a Reset by God; they were no longer slaves, but free now. They were no longer financially broke but abundantly blessed. They were no longer victims but victors over Egypt. But when pressure came, they reverted back to a negative attitude. Sure, the land is what God said, but...

"But" is a marker of personal decision on how we will interpret the circumstance.

The land is what God said, but there are giants there, there are fortified cities and we are very small and that is how they see us.

Or, the land is what God said and sure, there are challenges there in front of us, but God is able to help us through whatever we face because God already did so many miracles on the journey to here.

Both the hummingbird and the vulture fly over our nation's deserts. All vultures see is rotting meat, because that is what they look for. They thrive on that diet. But hummingbirds ignore the smelly flesh of dead animals. Instead, they look for the colorful blossoms of desert plants. The vultures live on what was. They live on the past. They fill themselves with what is dead and gone. But hummingbirds live on what is. They seek new life. They fill themselves with freshness and life. Each bird finds what it is looking for.

What are you looking for in this new season?

Dead things from the last season or freshness and life from this new season?

The story we just read goes on to say this:

Numbers 14:2 NLT

> *Their voices rose in a great chorus of protest against Moses and Aaron. "If only we had died in Egypt, or even here in the wilderness!"* **they complained.**

Complaining is the product and outward manifestation of a negative attitude.

A Negative attitude is an attitude marked by pessimism, cynicism, and a focus on the negative aspects of situations. A negative attitude can hinder performance, creativity, and collaboration, making it challenging to deliver consistent exceptional experiences. It can also create a toxic atmosphere that demoralizes team members and affects overall morale.

The Bible exhorts us to deal with our negative attitudes and not to let them develop into complaining.

Philippians 2:14 AMPC

> *Do all things without grumbling and fault-finding and complaining [against God] and questioning and doubting [among yourselves].*

Complaining has become a part of our everyday lives. We complain about traffic, politicians, athletes, entertainers, our spouses, our jobs, our children, our in-law and outlaws. We feel it is our right to complain frequently. We develop talk shows where they sit and complain about how someone is doing such a bad job. We watch sporting events, not good enough to play at that level ourselves, and complain about how they missed a shot, didn't catch a pass, struck out. We now have places in the newspaper to write our complaints to the editor. We have blurred the lines between healthy venting and unhealthy venting.

Tyler Jones, MD, chief medical officer at Banner Behavioral Health Hospital said, "When you're venting, you share your frustrations with someone you trust to reduce your stress. You're intentional about what you share and aware that you're venting. You may say something like, 'Can I just vent for five minutes?' expressing your dissatisfaction with the turn of events and looking to resolve those circumstances. Unhealthy venting is speaking out about everything to everyone because we feel like a victim, or we feel unable to change situations, so instead of finding constructive action to life we complain."

Studies have shown that complaining about your health actually tends to make your health worse.

Surely by now we have all heard of the placebo effect and know how it affects mind and muscle. A patient is given an inert pill (sugar pill) told that it may improve his/her condition, but not told that it is in fact inert. Such an intervention may cause the patient to believe the treatment will change his/her condition; and this belief may produce a subjective perception of a therapeutic effect, causing the patient to feel their condition has improved.

Upon further investigation, we realize that it wasn't the sugar pill that healed the person, so the question remains, "What healed him?"

I wasn't the sugar pill that healed him; he healed himself.

The human brain is simply amazing with its power. It can heal your body. What really healed the individual was his strong, unwavering belief that he would be healed. Even though he thought it was the pill healing him, he believed he would be healed.

There is an opposite reaction to this called the nocebo effect. This is, quite simply, the opposite of the placebo effect in that someone believes they won't be healed, regardless of what medicine they take or what steps they take to get better.

So how do we develop this "can-do" positive attitude?

First, be mindful of your self-talk.

Self-talk is what we say to ourselves inside our minds. How we talk to ourselves creates our experience. Our whole way of being, acting and feeling is influenced by how we talk to ourselves.

We speak **over 50,000 words** to ourselves each day in self-talk. That's an entire short novel we read to ourselves each day!

We can be mindful of our self-talk by keeping a pad of paper available to help us in the process. When we catch a piece of self-talk, write it down. For a week or two, just listen and catch your self-talk.

Second, change the narrative of your story.

You must replace the self-talk with the real truth. Caleb said, "Yes there are giants, but God is bigger than those giants." Your situation maybe sound like this: "Yes, they are laying people off, but if they lay me off, God will open another door of opportunity for me." Research shows that even a small shift in the way you talk to yourself can influence your ability to regulate your feelings, thoughts, and behavior under stress.

Try to imagine the best-case scenarios or focus on the good things that may happen in the future. This shift to optimism can help you have more positive expectations, which can lead to all sorts of good outcomes.

Thirdly, focus on strengths and positive qualities.

Make a list of your positive qualities. This will encourage you to move forward through risk and challenges with a sense of resilience. Reflecting on these can help you more easily focus on the good parts of yourself. This shift in focus can help us feel more positively about ourselves.

The noted English architect Sir Christopher Wren was supervising the construction of a magnificent cathedral in London. A journalist thought it would be interesting to interview some of the workers, so he chose three and asked them this question, "What are you doing?" The first replied, "I'm cutting stone for 10 shillings a day." The next answered, "I'm putting in 10 hours a day on this job." But the third said, "I'm helping Sir Christopher Wren construct one of London's greatest cathedrals."

Life is filled with ups and downs and unexpected turns. In this new season, you must intentionally decide not to let the past circumstances dictate your actions for today. A "can-do" attitude will approach each circumstance as a challenge to be solved, not an obstacle to stop us. This positive "can-do" attitude is what David put on to enter into his new season. The loss of yesterday is not the deciding factor for today. The mistakes of yesterday are not engraved in my future. The undervaluing of those around me and inside myself do not hinder my giftings and abilities to create something new! I am Reset, Repositioned, and Reclothed for what is ahead!

Bethany Hamilton is a professional surfer who lost her left arm in a shark attack when she was just 13 years old. Through Resetting and Repositioning her life, she was able to get back into the water and continue to pursue her passion for surfing and went on to win multiple competitions, including a national championship.

Two construction workers were eating lunch one day.

One of them says, "I hope I don't have another meat loaf sandwich. I'm getting tired of meatloaf."

The next day the construction worker opens his sandwich for lunch and says, "Meatloaf sandwich again! I hate this stuff!"

The third day this guy opens his lunch and says, "Oh, meatloaf again! I'm getting tired of this every day." The guy who's been eating lunch with him every day gets tired of hearing him complain and says, "Hey man, why don't you just get your wife to fix you a different kind of sandwich for lunch?'

The first guys replies, "My wife? What are you talking about? I'm not married! I make my own lunch."

You see, we are making our own lunches daily but we are complaining about what we are getting. We have the power to change it!

It is time to put on that "can-do" positive attitude and make ourselves something aligned with this new season we have entered into.

CHAPTER 11

A GENERATIONAL BLESSING

Through this whole process of Undervaluing or Loss or Failure, resetting his heart, repositioning his life and putting on new attitudes, David begins to understand the nature of God and God's plan and will for him.

David recognized this process (of resetting and repositioning) would require him to adapt a new life strategy and live that way from then on.

Many times, in the midst of this process we adopt a way of seeing things and our vision of the future becomes skewed. In this skewed vision we begin to think our best days are over, but this is so far from reality.

Jeremiah addresses this viewpoint to a group of people who thought this. They thought their past mistakes had set in motion difficult days and nothing could change that. Jeremiah encourages them that this is not true.

Lamentations 3:22-23 KJV:

The steadfast love of the LORD never ceas-

es; his mercies never come to an end; they are new every morning; great is your faithfulness.

The words steadfast love mean loyal love and generous favor. Here is the first amazing fact …even when we undervalue ourselves, lose something or someone, or mess up, God will still be committed by His love to fulfill His plan and purpose in our lives by His generous favor. This loyal love and generous favor from God never ceases. God is prompting, pushing us, confronting us to "reset" our hearts and "reposition" our lives so this loyal love and generous favor can accomplish His good pleasure ordain in our lives.

This is what David began to grasp and walk in.

Psalm 23:6 KJV:

Surely goodness and mercy shall follow me all the days of my life; and I will dwell in the house of the LORD forever.

David "Reset" his heart to be in tune with God.

"Even as pianos need constant tuning and regulating--not only when young and raw, but all through their careers of being used for brilliant concerts--so people who are being used as 'instruments of life'--or, in other words, living creative, fruitful lives--need constant refreshing, 'tuning.'" – Haddon Robinson

You and I need a constant "reset" to keep us in the rhythm of God for our lives.

David then "Repositioned" his life by repositioning his perception, thinking and emotions.

We often hear about exceptional winning streaks by teams, so what makes this winning streak by the Dayville High School girls' volleyball team in Oregon unique? Dayville ran off a string of 65 victories before losing. What makes this streak so appealing is that Dayville High has only 18 girl students: 16 are on the volleyball squad and the 17th keeps score.

Although Dayville is one of the smallest Class B high schools in the state, it won the Class A volleyball championship for three years running. Part of its success must be due to its unbridled optimism. The letter that brought word of the winning streak said that after the defeat, "The team rebounded and has a winning streak of one."

After resetting and repositioning his life, David began to wear two new attitudes in his life: gratefulness and can-do positive attitude. They carried him to a new, unseen future with grace.

This process of Resetting took only seven days from start to finish. Let that sink in. It doesn't take a long time, but it has to be a whole-hearted, complete buy into the process. This whole process of Resetting, Repositioning, and Reclothing ends in such a beautiful way. It gives us a powerful truth and a blueprint in how to set in motion a blessing.

1 Samuel 12:24-25 NIV

> *Then David comforted his wife Bathsheba, and he went to her and made love to her. She gave birth to a son, and they named him Solomon. T8he LORD loved him; and because the LORD loved him, he sent word through Nathan the prophet to name him Jedidiah.*

When David walked through this process it set in motion a "generational blessing"!

The subject of blessing is mentioned in the Bible about 600 times. A blessing is a pronunciation which imparts spiritual power, opening the way for us in life, giving us approval and confidence, and power for us to succeed; it is grace to enable us to become what we are meant to become, and to achieve what we are meant to achieve. One which flows from one generation to the next, a generational blessing is that which passes from father to son, a blessing which, when carried by one generation, can and should be passed on to another.

The fruit of David allowing himself to Reset, Reposition and Reclothe himself released the fruit of his life to set up the next generation with the favor of God.

Please hear me. When you walk through this process and embrace the changes you need to make it not only releases you to a new future, it releases those around you and generations to come to walk in the favor of God.

Solomon did nothing, let that sink in, but be born of this new process. He is beneficiary of a Reset, Repositioned, Reclothed life. God loved him, but not only that God told the same prophet that brought David the confronting news that put David on the path walk through this process, to now go tell David to rename his son. The name Jedidiah means "beloved of God."

There is something so powerful here. As you have found yourself somewhere in this journey with me and you have walked through this process with me, you recalibrated your life to a new future, with a new destination, to a wide-open place to flourish in your giftings and callings. You have also set in motion God's favor and love over the fruit of your life for generations to come, which is the result of your choices.

"When I was a boy, my father, a baker, introduced me to the wonders of song," tenor Luciano Pavarotti relates. "He urged me to work very hard to develop my voice. Arrigo Pola, a professional tenor in my hometown of Modena, Italy, took me as a pupil. I also enrolled in a teacher's college. On graduating, I asked my father, 'Shall I be a teacher or a singer?'

"'Luciano,' my father replied, 'if you try to sit on two chairs, you will fall between them. For life, you must choose one chair.'

"I chose one. It took seven years of study and frustration before I made my first professional appearance. It took another seven to reach the Metropolitan Opera. Choose one chair."

Now we see that our choices shape our future and the future of others. It is not what we have done, it is what we do next. Life will have messes, things will take a sudden change, we may lose people dear to us, or have to leave things behind that no longer fit, but when we make the right choices we open up a new future for ourselves and others. Generations to come benefit from our choosing wisely.

David's son Solomon was favored the moment he was born. Solomon went on to build the first permanent earthly house for God; we see a visible, tangible presence of God filling that house and shaping a nation. Solomon went on to set in motion a generational blessing for the next generation when he built this earthly house for God.

All this was set in motion by David's choice after his mistake. God is not limited by your losses, mistakes, and undervaluing. He is always faithfully waiting on you to move forward through this process.

It was my sophomore year of college and I had received several scholarships offers to notable colleges to play basketball. I had pursued a pathway in college to be a mechanical engineer. Several leading inventories I took in high school said this was what I would be gifted to do. After all, these expensive, up to date, and highly popular inventories couldn't be wrong. But my father watched me struggle to maintain a passion for this career, and I was making some bad choices along the way. I was all set to accept one of the scholarship offers when my father came in and had a talk with me. He said, "It doesn't appear that you are enjoying this career path, so I want to pay for you to go to a Bible school for a year in Dallas." I disagreed with him, because Bible school wasn't even on my horizon in any way. My father was a CPA, one of my grandfathers was a C banker, and the other one was a mechanical engineer. My life was being "Reset" and I didn't even know it.

After a year at Bible college, I began to feel to feel a shift. After the second year at Bible college, I felt this was what I was created to do. After I graduated, I entered into youth ministry, became an associate, a worship pastor, a senior pastor, and the rest is still playing out in my life. Years later I have been married to an amazing woman, we have six beautiful children. Five of them serve in the life of a local church and three of them are married as I am writing this. When my father "Reset" my life it set in motion a generational blessing over his grandchildren, and even though he is gone, that blessing is still reaping huge dividends. God is a generational God, moving you through life and all the changes you will need to make to reach your final destination. Resetting, Repositioning, and Reclothing will happen many times in your life. I have been through this process many times: a move from California to Arizona, a move to become an educator while still being a minister, a move to pioneer our own church, and many others. Full disclosure. I am walking through this process as this book is being written.

Thousands of years after his death,, in the New Testament, God refers to David in this manner:

And when He had removed him, He raised up

David to be their king: of him He testified and said, 'I HAVE FOUND DAVID the son of Jesse, A MAN AFTER MY OWN HEART [conforming to My will and purposes], who will do all My will.'

— **Act 13:22 AMP**

David had been undervalued, so he Reset his life. David had messed up, a couple of times, so he Reset his life. David had suffered loss, the loss of his kingdom, the loss of his son, so he Reset his life. David learned that in life things will happen; you will be undervalued and you will outgrow other peoples' opinion of your gifts and callings, you will suffer unexpected loss of career and loved ones, you will mess up, probably more than once. So know that Reset and walking through the process is how you move forward into the wide open space of God's future for you. That is why God called him "a man after my own heart." Nothing will stop the man or woman who has learned this valuable lesson. A Reset, Repositioned, Reclothed life is the best life to live!

I encourage you to embrace the process; even though it is scary, unknown, unfamiliar and unwritten it is still the greatest choice you will make, so make it over and over again. In making the choice you will change the course of your life and the lives of your loved ones to come.

In December of last year (2012) NPR told the story of a poor community in Paraguay which has formed an amazing orchestra that plays instruments created from recycled trash. The young musicians live in a slum that's built on a landfill. More than 1,500 tons of trash get dumped into the landfill every day. About 1,000 residents make their living by picking through the trash with long hooks called ganchos (hence the garbage pickers are called gancheros). Favio Chavez, a young professional and musician, and Luis Szaran, a music conductor, have infused the landfill with warmth, dignity, and beauty. When Chavez saw the desperate poverty and dire health conditions at the landfill, he opened a tiny music school. He asked one of the trash-pickers, Nicolas Gomez, to make some instruments from recycled materials. Eventually the students learned to play in a small orchestra of miraculously redeemed instruments: a cello made out of an oil can and old cooking tools, a flute made from tin cans, a drum set that uses X-rays as the skins, bottle caps that serve as the keys for a saxophone, a double bass constructed out of chemical cans, and a violin made from a battered aluminum salad bowl and strings tuned with forks. The "Recycled Orchestra" plays classical music, Paraguayan folk tunes, and even a few rock pieces. This story reminds us that nothing is as it seems, but with vision and follow through amazing things can happen to us and through us for generations to come.

So here is to your journey. May you be filled with grace and patience as you Reset your life and Reset your future.

Printed in the USA
CPSIA information can be obtained
at www.ICGtesting.com
LVHW021324200324
774923LV00008B/152

9 798890 417503